WINNING
FORMULAS

WINNING FORMULAS

STELLA OLADIRAN

authorHOUSE®

AuthorHouse™
1663 Liberty Drive
Bloomington, IN 47403
www.authorhouse.com
Phone: 1-800-839-8640

First published by AuthorHouse   12/14/2011

ISBN: 978-1-4567-8139-2 (sc)
ISBN: 978-1-4567-8138-5 (ebk)

Printed in the United States of America

DEDICATION

This book is dedicated to the Almighty God,
my source of inspiration.

The God that never fails. The God of wonders.

CONTENTS

INTRODUCTION

When you have a headache, the medicine the doctor prescribes is most likely to be different from that given to you, when you had a stomach upset. So also, in life, the problem you maybe facing right now, could be quite different from the one you had six months ago.

Just as we have physical prescription, so also do we need divine prescriptions: words of wisdom and knowledge, to help us in solving the various, physical emotional and spiritual conflicts of life. This book is a collection of winning strategies in various aspects of life

This is a collection of various articles written by me, spanning a period of ten years, divinely inspired to touch almost every aspect of your lives. Just as you consult your physician in times of physical ailment, so should you consult this book frequently, by going through the index to identify which article best suit your purpose at any point in time. Therefore, this book is recommended to all who want to live a victorious and excellent life as a 'keep sake' not just a "once reading", but a 'must have' in your quest to live a successful life. Behold, your "Winning Formulars"

IMPATIENCE THE BANE OF BLESSINGS

THERE ARE INHERENT DANGERS IN BEING HABITUALLY IMPATIENT EVEN AS A CHILD OF GOD.

"Be patient!" How many times have you heard this sound advise from someone and you become even more impatient. It is not easy, but the fact remains that, for us to have the best that we desire in life, most times we just have to exercise this wonderful virtue called patience. Failure to do so, may mean losing out on so many special blessings in life, whereas it is the Lords will that we should prosper in every area of our lives (3 John 1 :2) Everyone loves to be a winner, nobody wants to lose, but are we all ready to persevere in order to be the best that God wants us to be? Ask that Olympic gold medallist, and he would tell you how long and vigorous he had to prepare before he became a champion. Ask that Army General, Managing directors of multinational companies, banks, General overseer of mega churches and they will all have so much to tell you concerning how they reached their present exalted position. Good success is never instant, it takes hard work, good planning, patience and of course, good relationship with God who make all things beautiful (Eccl 3: 11)

So many people are living far below God' expectation for their lives, not because they lack the ability to excel, but due to their inability to wait on God to help them achieve their heart's desire. As such they settle for whatever is available and at times even give up on their dreams. This is why you see some people in wrong professions today, because they were not patient enough to secure admission and read the course of their dreams. And even those who read desired courses could not withstand the delay in getting related jobs. As a result they move from one job or vocation to another in search of prosperity and job satisfaction. Similarly, some people have ended up with the wrong marriage partners due to pressure from family and friends and their inability to persevere and allow God to give them his own choice. Do not be deceived by the devices of the devil. His plans are always to rob the Children of God of all the great benefits (Ps 68: 19) that God has for them in order to ensure that they lives a mediocre live on earth instead of the glorious lives they were destined for.

DANGERS OF IMPATIENCE

There are inherent dangers in being habitually impatient even as a child of God. Mind you, there is a trace of impatience in every human being. Everyone gets impatient with someone, certain situation at one point or another, but the level you allow your impatient to deteriorate to, will determine the danger inherent. It can start with everyday occurrence. For instance some people cannot endure the simple chaos of waiting for bus at the bus stops. Instead of waiting patiently like others, they start hissing, cursing and even at times forgo their journey. In most cases, the moment they leave, a bus arrives and they miss their appointment, which could have been beneficial to them. Some people cannot just imagine themselves queuing up to get something, they take one look at the queue and decide to postpone whatever they had to do, in the process delaying their blessings. Remember, that procrastination is the thief of time.

In the same vain, some housewives get themselves worked up unnecessarily over any delay in their husband's returning back from work. They get so agitated that when he eventually arrives, instead of the warm welcome he envisaged, all he encounter his anger and accusations from his wife. This behavior will invariably leads to friction in the marriage.

Gradually, this impatience builds up to other more important aspect of their lives. Some people find it difficult to know that they need to wait on God for certain blessings to manifest in their lives. The "I must have it now" syndrome dominate their consciousness always. That job, car, children, husband must come now. In the process, some manipulate others, tell lies and do devious things in order to achieve their aims. Remember, what you do not receive through the right way will not last. 'The blessing of god maketh rich and add no sorrow to it" (Prov 10:22)

Some Christians also loose their salvation as a result of impatience. The scripture emphatically told us to seek the kingdom of God and his righteousness and all other things will be added unto us (Matt 6:33) (Money, spouse, job, cars, whatever we need). The lord has also promised to give us anything we need (Phil 4:19), but we have a part to play. We must first of all know Him intimately as a child knows his father. Then we must have absolute faith in him and then wait patiently for the fulfilment of his promises in our lives. We are all encourage to be like Abraham, who after he had patiently endured, he obtained the promise of God for his life (Heb6:15)

HOW TO DESIGN FOR YOUR BLESSINGS

(i)   Whatever you are asking God to do for you, certainly has to be worth waiting for. Do not compare yourself with others. Unnecessary comparison can lead to envy and sometimes bitterness. Some people compare themselves to their former classmates who have since become owners of cars, houses while they are still managing in their present salary. There is nothing wrong in being ambitious and aiming to better your life, but when all you see is the. success of others and how you have been left behind, you might not have the peace and wisdom to make a success of your own life. That success story of your brother, friend, neigbhour should inspire you to do better, it should not be a reference point for your lack of patience and desperation to have what you want at all cost. Everyone has his/her own time; the people you think have overtaken you today might be behind you tomorrow as long as you allow God to have His way in your life.

(ii)   Time of waiting should be a time of preparation for higher responsibility. When you eventually get that multimillion-naira contract how would you handle the money? Will you still be close to God as you are today? When you eventually get that man/woman of your dream how Can you make your marriage an enjoyable one? At times, God deliberately allow certain blessings to be delayed in our lives in order to prepare us ready for the responsibilities that comes with it. For instance, if you are-a compulsive spender the Lord might not allow you to have that million now so that you do not squander it away. You have to learn to manage and appreciate its value before he releases the money into

4

your hands. Believe it or not, Joseph's travail in Egypt was a preparation for him becoming the second in command to Pharaoh. If he had not endured, how would he have reached that exalted position? (Gen. 41:40).

(iii)   During the period of waiting for that special blessing, you must be busy dong things that will please God and enhance your life. Get more involve with God's work, preach the good news, work in the Lord's vineyard and of course be obedient to God's word. This will not only enhance your spiritual life but gives you the strength you need to wait upon the Lord. Similarly, waiting for a spiritual blessing does not mean that you have to put your physical life on hold. There is always room for improvement. Get more education, enroll for that vocational training you have always been interested in. For instance a woman waiting on the Lord for the fruit of the womb can enroll in any sewing institute to know how to design and make good clothes for herself and family in the future.

You do not have to mop around all day just waiting for the miracle to manifest. In addition keep yourself neat and smart. Do not allow your problem to mirror on your face; everyone you see out there has his or her own problem. If it was possible to see through everyone's heart you will be amazed at what pain that gaily dressed and eversmiling lady is passing through.

IMPATIENCE

Remember, the Lord has told us to be of good cheer, because He has already overcomes the world (John16:33). In addition, encourage yourself in the Lord. The period of waiting for special blessings is always prone to depression that if care is not taken one may derail from God and loose not only those things he desires but even the one he already had. We must be like David, who encouraged himself in the Lord continually (Psalms). This was one of the secrets of his success. In that moment of depression, sing praises to God, read the scriptures. Locate the particular portion that is pertains to what you are going through and meditate on it. Use the word of God to pray concerning your situation. If you rely on other people to encourage you always, you might be disappointed because even those very close to you have their own lives to live and their own peculiar problems. Guide against the tendency to go running from one individual to another seeking their advice and support in every problem you face. Man is limited; they can only help you as far as their human ability allow them. Your limitless help can only come from God. (Psalms 121)

NOW MAKE YOUR CHOICE

God created us with a mind and a will so that we are free to make choices. You therefore have the right to choose to be patient concerning your spiritual and physical blessings or decide otherwise. If you have made up your mind to be patient, then ask God for the strength and zeal not to give up half way. And if you decision is that you cannot continue to wait on God to provide certain things for you because of the delays you are encountering so be it. But do not blame anyone but yourself if you loose out in the end. Abraham had to wait till he was 100 years old before the promised child (Isaac) was born. It was his choice of going into Sarah's maid Hagar, even though Sarah initiated it that resulted in the birth of Ishmael. We are all aware of the conflict in the Middle East today, which is actually a conflict between the lineage of Isaac (Jews) and

Ismael. even in our individual lives, an honest examination will show you certain opportunities you missed as a result of impatience. In today's world where things are getting done faster and faster everyday, it is not easy to be patient. Teenagers are becoming graduates, youths below thirty are becoming millionaires, youths below thirty are becoming chief executives of companies, there is therefore the tendency to be impatient but remember that you cannot run faster than God. Patience is still an invaluable virtue we need in order to inherit God's promises in our lives. No wonder, the word of God's says, "For ye have need of patience, that after ye have done the will of God, ye might receive the promise. For yet a little while, and he that shall come will come, and will not tarry" (Heb. 10 36-37). It does not matter how modern the world has began, the principle of God remains. You cannot run before you crawl. Even Christ himself, Had to be born a child before he grew up and started his ministry on earth, even though he had been with God from the beginning of creation (John 1:1). Moreover, he waited till he was thirty years of age on earth before the commencement of his mission on earth. It is the same principle we must adopt as children of God, stop running faster than your legs can carry you, why should a young graduate of twenty-one years think that he must drive a flashy car now when he is still living under the roof of his parents. Take it easy, you will get your heart desires, but you must set your priorities right. Know what you want and work hard towards it. Do not see the little delays as a stumbling block; see it as a stepping-stone. Delay is not denial, except when you allow it to be. Be determined to overcome that mountain standing in your way of progress by steadfast prayers and obedience to God. If you refuse to give up, the enemy has no choice but to let go and you will receive your blessing. Finally, brethren examine yourself, are you easily prone to impatience or are you currently in a situation where you think that you have waited long enough for God to intervene? Then turn to the book of Joel, chapter 2, verses 19-27 and meditate extensively on what God has promised to do for those who wait on Him. Remember, they that wait upon the Lord shall never be ashamed.

BE STILL

To be still means to be calm, quiet with absolute faith, that God is in control no matter the situation. Brethren, we know it is not easy, particularly when faced with so many problems at the same time, and it seems as if the lord has deserted you. But it is exactly at this point that you need to be still because to do other wise would only compound the situation and you may end up losing.

The desire to write this article came at a very trying moment in my life when there seemed to be no solution in sight. And in the midst of it all, the Holy Spirit spoke the word 'Be still' into my spirit and that moment I experienced an indescribable peace that only God could give. No wonder it is written 'Be still and know that I am God, I will be exalted among the heathen, I will be exalted in the earth' [Psalm 46: 10].

This word of encouragement is very important because when trials come, especially in multiples as they do at times, there is the tendency to panic and weep, looking for solution where there is none there by prolonging the pain. A woman had been married for so many years without a child to show for it. As a result her in laws had started persecuting her in her matrimony home. To compound her problems her husband lost his job, due to that he changed his attitude towards her, instead of supporting his wife whenever his people came around to make trouble with· his wife, he became abusive and hostile. As a result she began to run from one place to another looking for solution.

No matter how terrible your case may be, it can never be worse than that of Job, who lost the entire things he had on the same day including his children. Yet he still rejoiced even when his wife asked him to curse God and die, hear what Job said· 'But he said unto her, thou speakest as one of the foolish, shall we receive good and not evil from God's hand. In all this Job did not sin (Job 2:10)

No matter what we may be going through in life, let us continue to lookup to Jesus with faith as Job did, remember Job did not only overcome, he was later blessed twice than he was before. [Job 42: 12]

At this junction, it is important to note that to be still, does not mean to be lazy, you won't do anything.

HOW NOT TO BE STILL

[i]   To be still does not mean a state of inaction when you do nothing waiting for God to intervene in your situation, rather you dwell in His presence by praying and fellowship with Him so that He can direct you to where your miracle awaits you.

(ii)   It is a time of Praise . . . and worship, time to declare' His wondrous works. Preach—the good news to others, tell them about the goodness of God in all situations, and you will be speaking mercy and favor into your life.

[iii]   This is the, period to take your God given blessing with force from the enemies' hand; Daniel had to wrestle in prayers for twenty one days until he took what belonged to him from the hand of the enemy (the Prince of Persia).

WHY YOU MUST BE STILL

[A]   Let God prove Himself in your situation, your problem can not be worse than that of the children of Israel in wilderness, even when God had proved Himself in the land of Egypt. They had thought that their problems were over; all they had to do was journey to the land God had promised them. But alas, it was not so. Staring at their faces was the red sea and there was no way they could pass through without getting drowned. To worsen the situation, behind them were the chariots and the horses of Pharaoh carrying soldiers in hot pursuit of them. (Ex. 14:9-10). Naturally, they panicked, accusing their leader Moses of bringing them on a suicide mission in the wilderness instead of allowing them to die in bondage in Egypt. They completely forgot, relegated to the background their years of travail in Egypt and how God brought them out after signs and wonders, including the various plagues and finally the slaying of every first born child of the Egyptian. (Ex 12: 2a) But Moses instead of crying like the others turned to the almighty God for solution and spoke words of encouragement to the people. And Moses said unto the people; fear not stand still and see the salvation of the Lord, which he will show you today. For the Egyptians whom ye have seen today, ye shall see them no more forever' [Ex 14: 13]. In their panic, they could have done more harm to themselves even before the soldiers of Pharaoh got to them. It is the same thing that is happening to us.

No matter how terrible the problem seems, God wants to prove himself in our lives. Moses encouraged the people of Israel to remember how God parted the Red sea for them at the point of hopelessness. God is still the same, He never changes. Whatever the situation allow Him to have his way, all you need do is to act according to his word' For thus saith the Lord God, the Holy one of Israel, in returning and rest shall ye be saved; in quietness and in confident shall be your strength and ye would not' [Isaiah 30: 15]

[b]   The battle is not yours even as you face different battles everyday 'seen and unseen'. This battle may come in a small or a big way, don't say you can handle it yourself, handover all battles to God right from the start. Let Him know that you cannot help yourself, God is our refuge and strength, a very present help in trouble. With Him on your side you are sure of victory.

[c]   It is when you are calm you are likely to have clearer insight of any situation you may be going through in life, most times people see their problems as very big in their mind which make pathways for the devil to manage the situation for them. You should not allow anxiety and fear to overwhelm you, but understand the plan of God for you therefore have confidence in God who is able to give you victory in any battle of life.

When you are still in the midst of 'storm' you will be able to hear and obey the voice of God, your miracle may just be around the corner.

CAN YOU GET ANGRY WITH GOD?

Oh God, why are you allowing this thing to happen to me? What have I done to deserve all these? Have you ever had cause to utter these or similar statements, watch out! You may have been angry with your Maker without been aware of it. Some people may even argue that there is nothing wrong in being angry with Him after all He is our Father. Well there is nothing wrong with a child being angry with his father when the father has deliberately offended him. But God can do no wrong. He is immortal God, infallible God. He says that His thoughts towards us are of peace, not evil to give us an expected end (Jer. 29: 11). God does not cause us pain, as a matter of fact he heals our pains, our wounds, whether physical or emotional.

God cannot hate His children, He loves them, for God is love. (1st John 4:8). It is only someone who hates you and is really wicked that can deliberately inflict so much pain on you and that person is Satan, the author of wickedness. The word of God says that "The thief cometh not, but for to steal, and to kill, and to destroy". That thief is Satan.

Therefore when you are going through these terrible trials and temptation, never, never direct your anger at God, direct it to the author of the problem—the devil.

The problem with many people, even born-again children of God is that they are not conscious of the fact that Satan is responsible for the various woes they are encountering in their lives even after surrendering their lives to Jesus Christ. It is he that is responsible for your not getting a job years after graduation. He is responsible for the breakage of some marriage after years of marital bliss. Satan is responsible for the downturn of some once thriving business. He is the one who does not want some to even marry so that his agents can mock them. In fact, Satan is responsible for the countless negative situations bedevilling many children of God. That is his work. He never want anything good to come to you. He. carries out his evil activities through his various categories of agents scattered all over the world. No wonder the scripture says that "For we wrestle not against flesh and blood, but against principalities, powers, against the rulers of the darkness of this world, against spiritual wickedness in high places". Eph. 6:12. Now that you know the enemy, your problem is already half solved.

GET ANGRY WITH THE SITUATION

What is that problem that has caused you so much pain? Nearly exhausted your spiritual and physical strength and almost cause you to rebel against God through anger?

Do not be like the children of Israel who murmured against their God in the wilderness out of frustration, only to loose the promise of God in their lives. (Exod. 14:11-12, Exod. 16:3). Despite the mighty miracles God performed in their midst in Egypt and after bringing them out of bondage, at the slightest discomfort, they rebelled against God and Moses. Many Christians are still like that today, a minor problem is enough for them to threaten to go back to the world and do as they like. The truth is that God never promised us a problem—free world. The fact that you are a child of God does not mean that Satan will leave you alone. On the contrary, this is when he is more interested in you because you have been snatched from him, out of the kingdom of darkness. He hates to loose anyone because he wants many people to perish with him in hell.

But we have been assured that in all of Satan's roaring and plotting of evils, that we are more than conquerors through Jesus Christ who loves us (Rom. 8:37). So, tell that bareness in your life (bareness is not of women alone) be it financial, spiritual, physical that its reign in your life is over. You have a covenant of faithfulness with your God. "And God blessed them, and God said unto them, be fruitful and multiply and replenish the earth, and subdue it and have dominion over the fish of the sea, and over the foul of the air, and over every living thing that moveth upon the earth". Gen. 1:28. God created us to have dominion over every situation in life and this should be the attitude of every believer.

USE THE WORD OF GOD

"In the beginning was the word, and the word was with God, and the word was God". John I: I. Jesus Christ is the word of God. Is there any more potent weapon of warfare than the king of kings and the Lord of Lords himself? The Jehovah, the Man of war (Exod. 1 S :38). Some people can lock themselves up in a room for hours reading one romantic or action novel, but give then the bible to dwell upon, in the next few minutes it is closed. Then they are still wondering why the enemy torments them regularly despite the fact that they are regular church goers. It is not attending church alone that matters, you must have the word of God (Christ) inside of you to do the battle. What you do not have, you cannot use. This is why you discover that at the slightest battle you are easily overwhelmed because you do not have the power of inside of you. "For the word of

God is quick and powerful, and sharper than any two edged sword . . ." (Heb. 4: 12). Everyday we are engaged in warfare, seen and unseen, whether we know it or not. You must be prepared at all times to defeat the enemy and one sure weapon of victory is the infallible word of God (Joshua 1 :8).

BE DETERMINED TO OVERCOME THE SITUATION

Sweet victories over negative situations come to those who are determined to overcome them. You must come to the point when you completely reject that yoke or reproach in your life and say no more. Some people behave as if they enjoy certain problems. Some of them even use such problems as escape routes from taking on certain responsibilities. What a shame! For instance a man lost his job and he is still looking for another, after two years; instead of mapping out strategies of either getting another job or embarking on a small scale business, he start pitying himself and complaining to anyone who cares to listen of how life has treated him badly. This will not solve the problem. Remember others have been in similar situation before you and they overcame. You too can overcome your present predicament. Rev. 12: 11 says "And they overcome him by the blood of the lamb, and by the word of their testimony": God is able to turn it around for good. For the word of God says that "the silver is mine and the gold is mine, saith the Lord of hosts" Haggai 2:8.

"The Lord shall open unto thee his good treasure, the heaven to give thee rain unto thy land in his season, and to bless all the work of thine hand, and thou shall lend into many nations, and thou shall not borrow" Deut. 28: 12. If only we can be patient and obedient to the word of God and tap into his wonderful promises for us, most of the sufferings we encounter would never happen.

I surrendered my life to Christ years ago in a church which had a department with the above name (PUSH UNIT)—Pray until something happen. It epitomises the extent to which we Christians should pray. We must never be tired of praying no matter how long we have been praying over a particular situation II Thess. 5: 17 says "Pray without ceasing"

These are various reasons for the unseemingly unanswered prayers in our lives. God may have had actually granted your request long ago but the enemy Satan is resisting your reception of the blessing. This was what happened to Daniel when the enemy, the Prince of Persia resisted his blessing for twenty-one days until an angel intervened and brought down the miracle to him. (Dan. 10: 12-13). It took prayers to have his problems solved, and it was also prayers that delivered the blessing to Daniel. This type of situation is still manifesting in the world today. In addition, we must also learn to pray in accordance with the will of God. It's of no use weeping, just because you have been praying for years to have a particular blessing, and no result. God who sees tomorrow from today may actually be saving you from an unseen failure. Just change your prayer line to "God, please give . . . in your own time, and He will surely give you the best because He is a giver of every good and perfect gift. (James 1: 17). Brethren you should never be tired of praying. Be like Jacob who wrestled with an angel all night and would not let him go until he had blessed him "And he said, let me go, for the day breaketh. And he said, "I will not let thee go, except thou bless me". Gen. 32:26. So, brighten that lovely countenance of yours, **HE cares**

BE HAPPY NOW!

One basic need that is universal to every man is the desire to be happy. But many people forfeit their joy by putting their lives on hold until conditions become perfect.

Instead of being happy and grateful to God for what they have achieved so far, many deny themselves of the inner joy they could have, by waiting for the time they will have the ideal job, prosperous business, comfortable home, life partner, children or any other needs they may have. This is why there is so much frustration in the lives of some people, even born again children of God, who should know better. We must realize that our happiness depends on God and not on man or situations. This is why the scriptures clearly tells us in Phil. 4:4 to rejoice in the Lord always. We are not to rejoice in our achievements, but in the LORD. There are many situations which may cause men to forfeit their joy. As our faces vary, so do the problems we face individually. In fact every face tells a different story. We shall try to analyze some common situations which may make many people suspend their joy.

LACK OF JOB SATISFACTION

There are many people out there, who though have the jobs that others are searching for, are still very discouraged because they have not attained the very desire of their hearts. Their usual song is this "Well I am just managing this for now. My dream is to work in the oil industry, bank, etc." They have forgotten to thank God and appreciate the job He has given them at the

moment. There is nothing wrong with having an ambition and wanting to have the very best. In fact, that should be the desire of everyone. However you must not look down on that job that currently puts food on your table, just because you are aiming for something higher. Some people even go to the extent of developing a lukewarm attitude towards their jobs, thereby. denying their employers the best of their abilities. Instead of doing the jobs they are being paid for, they grumble incessantly and tell everyone who cares to listen that they are not happy with their jobs. If Elisha had despised his job as Elijah's servant, he would never have had the honour of being Elijah's successor (II Kings 2: 15). Despite Joseph's position as a servant in the house of Potiphar and subsequently as a prisoner. he always maintained a cheerful disposition and performed his duties creditably. This later earned him the exalted position of the second-in-command to Pharaoh in Egypt. No wonder. Apostle Paul says in I Thess. 5: 18 "In everything give thanks:
 for this is the will of God in Christ Jesus concerning you". The secret is that when you appreciate and thank God for the little you have today, he will do more for you. that will even surpass your dream.

UNPROFITABlE BUSINESS

It is common knowledge that the economic situation in the country has not been favourable to many businesses in the last decade. That notwithstanding, you should still rejoice in the LORD always, knowing that He has promised never to leave you nor forsake you. Instead of grumbling and making yourself and your loved ones miserable because of the downturn of your once profitable business, commit everything unto the hands of God and let Him be the boss in all your ventures. After all the Almighty God has promised in Psalm 32:8 "I will instruct thee and teach thee in the way which thou shalt go: I will guide thee with mine eyes". The problem with many of us is that we do not wait for instruction from God before embarking on any business.

Even after we start a business. we still refuse to allow the Spirit of God to lead us.' Instead we choose to rely on our own human intelligence and earthly connections alone. We tend to go after any business that is in vogue. If others are into fashion designing. we go into it: tomorrow it may be food-related business, the next time, it maybe sales. Some run from one city to another, from one influential uncle to another, looking for nonexistent big contracts that will fetch millions at a time. When there seems to be no headway, frustration sets in and robs them of their joy. This sometimes affects their families. and accounts for why some men who were once loving fathers and husbands, suddenly become tyrants at home.

If you are presently in this situation. all hope is not lost. Determine in your heart now that you are going to get out of this negative situation through God's help. Zech. 4:6 says: "Not by might. Nor by power, but by my spirit. says the Lord of hosts." Let me remind you of what the word of God says about those who put their trust in man "Thus saith the Lord. cursed be to the man that tmsteth in man, and maketh flesh his arm, and whose heart departeth from the LORD. For he shall be like the heath in the desert, and shall not see when good cometh; but shall inhabit the parched places in the wilderness, in a salt land and not inhabited", (Jer. 17:5-6). Conceming those who put their trust in God, the reverse is the case. "Blessed is the man that trusteth in the LORD, and whose hope the LORD is. For he shall be as a tree planted by the waters, and that spreadeth out her roots by the river, and shall not see when heat cometh, but her leaf shall be green; and shall not be careful in the year of drought, neither shall cease from yielding fruit". (Jer. 17:7-8). No matter the setback you may have experienced in your business, do not allow the enemy to steal your joy. Hab. 3:17-19. Instead, re-dedicate your business to God, and allow Him to lead and guide you. With patience and hard work, your business will not only bounce back to life, but will surpass the magnitude of the past. Our God is limitless.

THE UNMARRIED SISTER/BROTHER.

From my own observations, I have come to the conclusion that this is the largest group of people who, on their own volition. have decided to suspend their joy until their situation changes. This is especially true for the unmarried sister. The commonest reason being that most of their friends and mates are already married, while she is yet to get a proposal from the man of her dreams. Instead of wallowing in self-pity, do something constructive now that will help to enhance your status later in life. If you have no job or trade, this is the time to get one and show commitment and diligence. If possible, go back to school and acquire more education in order to enhance your social and economic prospects. Above all, busy yourself doing the work of God both within the house of God and wherever you may find yourself.

We must realise that God created each one of us individually, for a specific purpose. The fact that your younger sister got married two years ago while you are still single, does not mean that God does not love you. This reminds me of the testimony of a lady I know very well. Many years ago, after completing her university education, she got a very good job. Even that did not really impress her relatives, who felt that she was over due for marriage, because her younger sister had since married.

They mounted pressure on her to get married even after she had explained to them that she had not met the right man. Instead of allowing this situation to depress her and steal her joy, she decided to go back to school on a part-time basis, to get further professional qualification in order to enhance her career. Today she is not only a manager in her place of work, she is also happily married with two children.

To crown it all, her family and relatives now see her as a sort of pillar, because she has been able to help them out in times of financial crises. They are now proud of her. Even her younger sister (who got married before her), sometimes comes to her for financial assistance, because in her haste to get married, she neither acquired a higher education nor trained for any vocation.

As we all know, the economic situation of today does not make, for a wife to be totally dependent on her husband financially. She must make her own contributions towards the family's upkeep, no matter how little. The fact that you are not married today does not mean that it will not happen tomorrow. Don't put your happiness on hold, waiting for that day. Be happy now. God is preparing you for your role as a wife or husband. Afterall, He did say that, it is not good for man to be alone (Gen. 2: 18). Your own role in the mean time is to prepare yourself physically, for marriage, by taking good care of yourself. Some sisters are inconsistent in this regard, today they may look neat and smart, tomorrow they look so untidy that people may see them and immediately conclude they have a problem. Prepare yourself economically by being gainfully employed or involved in a trade or business. Above all, prepare yourself spiritually. Marriage is serious business, you need God to make it work and be fulfilling. Allow God to choose your partner for you. Remember that marriage is not the end of everything in life, it is just the beginning of another phase in one's life. If you refuse to be happy now because you are not married, chances are that you might still not be happy when you eventually get married. Please relax and let God work out everything for you. If you consider your single status a reproach, ask God to remove it from you (Joshua 5:9), and He will surely answer you. Afterall, our God has promised that His people will never be ashamed (Joel 2:25-27).

MARRIED COUPLES SEEKING THE FRUIT OF THE WOMB

Are you unhappy in your marriage because there are no kids yet? Some couples create unnecessary strains in their marital relationship, just because they are not patient enough to wait on the LORD to bless them with children. If God in His infinite wisdom has given you a life partner, He will surely bless your marriage with children at the appointed time. Remember, it is written in Phil. 1:6, "Being confident of this very thing, that He which hath begun a good work in you will perform it until the day of Jesus Christ"

The problem however, is that some couples are not prepared to wait on the the Lord. Instead, they choose to live in their own separate agonies and make each other miserable, rather' than allow the negative situation to bring them closer to themselves, and to God. Such couples should use the time to draw strength from each other and from God. and then confront whatever is responsible for the delay in having children. Our Lord Jesus Christ tells is in Matt. 18: 19 "that if two shall agree on earth as touching anything that they shall ask. It shall be done for them of our father which is in heaven. Do not alloew any situation to steal your joy. Depression is a hindrance to faith. This is the time to have absolute faith in God, in His ability to do what He has said He would do.

In conclusion, we must imbibe the habit of being happy always regardless of the situation we find ourselves in. As Christians, circumstances or situations should not determine our state of happiness. Never suspend your joy until you attain a certain position or a particular need is met. Otherwise you may go through life without knowing the real joy of living. This is because as long as we are alive, needs will always arise. and circumstances will always change. The good news is that when you become rooted and grounded in the word of God. the joy of the Lord will be your strength at all times. A joyful heart gives thanks. When we learn to appreciate and thank God for who we are and what we have achieved today, He will surprise us by blessing us beyond our expectations. "For He is able to do exceeding abundantly above all that we ask or think. according to the power that worketh in us" (Eph. 3:20).

Remain blessed in Jesus name. AMEN

WAITING

Waiting for the promises of God to manifest can be a very trying time for the believer. It is also a time of great temptation; that if care is not taken, the person involved may be led astray and may even miss the promise. How does one handle such a situation? Habakkuk. 2:3 tells us that; "For the vision is yet for an appointed time, but at the end it shall speak, and not lie: though it tarry, wait for it; because it will surely come, it will not tarry".

As human beings, waiting for anything is not easy. Even everyday occurrences such as waiting for someone to show up for an appointment; waiting for a bus to arrive at the bus stop; waiting for a relative or friend to fulfill a certain promise can be very tasking. Therefore waiting for the promises of God which cannot be seen requires a lot of patience and total reliance on the word of God. Rom. 8:25 says; "If we hope for that we see not, then do we with patience wait for it". we have also been assured in Num. 23:19 that 'God is not man that he should lie neither the son of man that he should repent; hath he said, and shall he not do it? or hath he spoken, and shall not make it good?"

What is it that God has promised you? Is it a child, a good job, healing, husband or peace in your home? Whatever it is, as long as God has promised you, it will surely come to pass. Fix your eyes on the promise and not on the problems you may encounter before obtaining the promise. Problems will always come, obstacles may come, after all God did not promise us a problem_ free world, but He did say that we shall overcome by the blood of the lamb and the words of our testimony. And God also says in Heb. 10:36 that; "For ye have need of patience that, after ye have done the will of God, ye might receive the promise". Abraham endured and he obtained his promise. And today testimonies abound of men and women who persevered when faced within many obstacles and in the end, obtained God's promise.

God demonstrated to us the high regard He has for endurance when He allowed His only begotten Son, Jesus Christ to suffer a lot of persecution in the hands of the Jews and died on the cross for the redemption of our sins. And for this reason Christ received His own reward from God because it is written in Phil. 2:9-10 "Wherefore God also hath highly exalted him and given him a name which is above every name. That at the name of Jesus every knee should bow, of things in heaven and things on earth and things under the earth"

If our Lord Jesus, the Son of God could be rewarded for His steadfast endurance then we are assured that God will reward us with the manifestation of whatever He has promised us. All we need to do is to ask the Lord to give us the strength to sail through during the time of waiting for the promise; by steadfast prayers, meditation on the word of God and complete obedience to His word. And at the end we would obtain the promise. After all Zech. 4:6 says "Not by might, nor by power but by my spirit, saith the Lord of hosts". Therefore, remind God of His promises to you and, patiently wait upon the Lord of hosts in prayer, meditate on his word, and let obedience be your watch word. At the appointed time of God, you will obtain the promise. Halleluyah!

BETTER IS THE END

It is not enough to have a good start in any endeavor of life, but more importantly it is how we can sustain it and end it well. Many people are good starters but poor finishers. They begin the year well, with wonderful resolutions, they start their Christian race well, with so much zeal to serve God, they begin a job with so much dedication to duty; alas!

Midway, they change completely. The resolutions, the fervency to serve the Lord the wonderful relationships are discarded. Meanwhile their expectations remains. They still desire the best from the Lord; they still want to attain the highest position in their places of work and of course, the best in their relationships. It is not possible, you must give, in order to receive. It is the best that you give out of yourself—your service, talent, love and time that will determine what you will receive in return, or how far you can go in the ladder of success. (Luke 6:28).

Some people attribute every failure in their lives to satan, well it cannot be ruled out. But there are many things we fail to achieve in life due to our own making. It is either we refuse to contribute our own quota to the success of that venture or as in most cases, we begin well, but give up half—way due to negligence or lack of patience to endure the pain which always lead to gain. No wonder the word of God says that "Better is the end of a thing than the beginning thereof: and the proud in spirit is better than the period in spirit"(Ecclesiastes. 7:8)

FACTORS RESPONSIBLE FOR
POOR FINISHING

INCONSISTENCY

Some people are so fickle minded that you begin to wonder whether they realize that there is an innate strength given to us Christians at the time of our salvation. One day they portray someone of high integrity and the next day it is a different story entirely. For instance a child of God begins a good job with the determination and zeal to excel. But as usual, he discovers that there are few problems, which is normal in any success venture. First he discovers that it is not everybody that shares the same principle of transparency and dedication to duty with him. In fact some of his colleagues have even started to castigate him for being over zealous as far as they are concerned and to remind him that the company does not belong to his father, as such he is expected to cooperate with them and defraud the company as much as they can. Instead of this Christian Brother remembering that the Lord had promised us, His children that no one can harm us if we are follower of that Which is good and that those who speak evil of us because we are doing good shall be ashamed (1 Peter 3:13-17) he foolishly renegade on his principle and decide to join the bandwagon of evil doers. Behold! The very first time he partakes in their evil activities, he is caught and his appointment terminated. Are you surprised? Don't you know that salvation makes the enemy to mark you out for destruction and the moment you fall into his trap, he strikes? It does not matter whether other people have been doing the same thing successfully, you are different from them because you are a child of God. Therefore brethren, we must be consistent in doing good no matter the opposition we face. Be rest assured that God will vindicate you and even those that condemn you now for doing good will commend you tomorrow, if you refuse to give up.

ii   LACK OF FOCUS

We must have a clear focus in every well thought out endeavor in life. There must be a purpose for that thing you want to do. For instance, what do you aim to achieve by becoming a born-again Christian? Is it just to follow the footstep of your friends or is it to have a good life on earth and make it to heaven eventually? What is your purpose of going into that profession, getting that job or venturing into that business? Is it just a temporal source of income or do you want to excel in it? If your aim is to excel, then you must realize that total dependence on God, hard work, diligence, discipline must be your watchword (Prov.22: 29). What is your purpose for getting married? Believe it or not, there are actually some people who do not have a clue as to why they got married. As far as they are concerned they were of marriageable age and therefore needed a spouse to complement them. The purpose of God for marriage is contained in the scriptures (Gen.2: 18,24,Ecc 4:9-11,1 Cor.7: 2-14). Do not be ignorant, be determined to know the purpose of God concerning marriage and let the same purpose guide you into making a success of your own marriage

iii **DISTRACTIONS:** Brethren there will always be distractions in life. We can never stop the eyes from seeing, the ear from hearing and the heart from feeling, afterall that is what they were created for. But how we handle the various distractions that arises in our quest for success will determine how far we go. For instance, distractions can come from what we hear from others, through advice or feedbacks. If you are the type who takes delight in asking for advice from every

"Tom, Dick and Harry" then you maybe plotting your own downfall unknowingly. Know the people you seek advise from concerning anything. They must be those who share the same vision with you concerning that situation. For instance a friend who did not want you to marry your wife will certainly not be the person to seek advise from when you have marital problems. Similarly, a person who is not a child of God as you are will surely not give you the godly advice that you need. Bear in mind that Jesus Christ is our ultimate counselor (Isaiah 9:6). Befriend Him and let Him guide you.

Some people are easily distracted by what they see happening around them. Today they see miracles taking place in a particular church and off they go. Tomorrow they see an advertisement of a "man of God" having a miracle crusade in so-so place and they rush there. They keep running form pillar to post looking for deliverance and miracle and at the end their case is worse off than before.

Channel your energy and time you use in running up and down to doing productive work both in the church where you worship and in your secular job and you will have course to smile at the end. (Mind you make sure you are part of a bible believing church where the word of God is preached without any addition or subtraction.)

For some people, distractions easily come through business. Today they are into one business and tomorrow they switch on to another just because they have seen someone prospering in that particular business. Before the end of the year, they would have tried at least five businesses without any appreciable success. Relax, locate your own vocation, and know what you want to do, plan well and pursue it with vigor. And with prayer and dedication you will surely succeed. For some, it is their feeling or emotions that are easily distracted.

One day they are at peace with everyone around them and the next it is malice galore. Any inconsequential thing is enough to offend them. It is not easy to focus on your desired goals when you keep malice and refuse to forgive your offenders. (Mark 11 :25) Exercise self-control even in the face of unjust persecutions. Allow God to fight your battles for you. Mind you, Satan will always try to use those closest to you to distract you from reaching your goals, so pray for them constantly and refuse to be provoked to anger unnecessarily.

Finally, for every good thing we have started in life, we must be determined to finish it well. Let your eyes be set on what you aim to achieve so that you will not be discouraged by the problems face. Let us be like the Olympic gold medallist,what he sees is himself crossing the finishing line, not in tears, not in second place, but with his hands raised up in VICTORY as he is declared the champion. That will be our portion in Jesus name. Amen.

COUNT YOUR BLESSINGS

Count your blessings! Name them one by one so says a popular song. If only most of us would remember this in our moments of depression and the usual trials of life. The truth is that some of us tend to overlook the common blessings we receive from God everyday and focus all our attention on those so-called special blessings that are yet to manifest in our lives. If that dream job has not materialize after two years of graduation from University; if the business is yet to pick up after years of struggling to build it; if that child is yet to come after several years of marriage, some erroneously believe that God has not blessed them. And you, my beautiful and hardworking sister who is yet to meet her 'Mr. Right' at thirty thinking that she has not achieved anything in life, despite her career and spiritual advancement.

Do you know that the miracle of your waking up this morning is a blessing? Even the mere fact that you are reading this message is a blessing, some would have loved to read but they can not because they have lost their sight. What of the fact that you have eaten at least a meal today, no matter how unpalatable it was; do you know that there are many people in hospitals who cannot even eat not because they cannot afford good food but because they are handicapped, and therefore cannot enjoy the sumptuous meals that you take for granted everyday. Some christians still bemoan their fate, complaining of every little discomfort in their lives, forgetting that there are other people in similar or worst situations. Remember what God says in I Cor. 10: 13 that, "there hath no temptation taken you but such as is common to man; but God is faithful, who will not suffer you to be tempted above that ye are able but will with the temptation also make a way to escape, that ye may be able to bear it."

Always bear in mind that you are not the only one, passing through that trial. In fact many have passed through it before you and come out triumphant.

Believe and know that God is in that situation with you. You are not alone. But you have your own part to play in order to escape from the situation. Your attitude and actions will determine whether you overcome or are overwhelmed by the trials you face.

For instance, despite the problem, you must still LOVE AND PRAISE GOD even in the midst of that situation. Some people wait for the manifestation of a miracle before truly praising God. If this is your attitude, you just have to change. Bear in mind that God blesses us everyday no matter how insignificant the blessing may seem to you. Psalm 68: 19 says "Blessed be the Lord, who daily loadeth us with benefits even the God of our salvation." So if you are still waiting for that special blessing to manifest before praising God, you are being ungrateful to

Him for the so called "little blessings" He gives to you daily. Moreover it is when you show appreciation for the so called little blessings that God will be pleased to perform the great ones in your life. Will you willingly increase the school allowance of a child who had shown contempt for the little money you could afford to give him in the past? You may still increase it because of your love for him but not willingly and certainly not with the amount that will really please him. So also is our God, He can still give us those blessings even when we do not deserve it but we know that praises and thanksgiving will hasten the manifestation of your blessings. A heart of gratitude and true worship will certainly provoke God to do greater things in our lives.

Secondly, STOP COMPLAINING and telling every sympathetic ear you problems. The fact is that if you are not contented and grateful to God for what you have at the moment, invariably you might complain. This is a very wrong step to take because a complaining heart and mouth only provoke God to anger and not to bless. Remember what happened to the children of Israel in the wilderness, a journey that was suppose to take them forty days lasted for fort years due to their disobedience an ingratitude to God (Deut. I :2). At the slightest discomfort, they murmured and rebelled against God and Moses.

A complaining heart is always full of bitterness. And bitterness can steal your joy and blind you to the truth concerning your situation. You become unable to focus properly and see a way out of your adversity because all you see and feel is what the enemy wants you to see, problems. Bitterness also saps you of the strength you derive from constant fellowship with the Lord. We must completely eschew bitterness in our lives

Thirdly, we also need PATIENCE in order to receive our spiritual blessings. Patience is a virtue we all require in order to excel in life, yet some people have come to regard it as a form of weakness. In this jet age where things are done very fast, some people cannot understand why we should wait for certain blessings to come to us through God alone when other people have used other means to get similar blessings in the past. Do you know what has happened to those people now? Moreover, know that you are unique and different from the other person. The fact that your neighbor visited a 'Spiritualist' who gave a concoction which she took and later conceived a child, does not mean that it will work for you too. Or that a 'good luck' charm given to your friend which enabled him to secure huge contracts will also work for you too. Don't you know that every good and perfect gift can only come from God? (James 1: 17. If the devil gives you anything no matter how good it may seem today it will certainly lead to deep sorrow sooner than later. Moreover, for anything the enemy (Satan) gives you, he takes away something more important from you. Would you rather have a child that will bring sorrow, and end to your marriage? Or wait patiently for God to give you the one that will be a great blessing to your family?

Finally, BE HAPPY NOW even before the blessings comes "Rejoice evermore. Pray without ceasing. In everything give thanks for this is the will of God in Christ Jesus concerning you." II Thess. 5: 16-18. Why should you suspend your joy just because you have a need that is yet to be met. As long as we live, there will always be a need, a desire per time. If you allow yourself to be depressed or caged in by the present problems of your life, you may never be happy. The end and beginning of the year is always a period of reflection and stocktaking for most people to determine the progress they have made in the past year. While some smile, others groan due to what they perceive as lack of achievement,others are happy. Anyway, it all depends on what you understand by the term achievement. If all you anticipated to do in the year have not manifested, please do not launch into despair. Instead focus on those things or areas where you have done well. Have you enjoyed a relatively good health this year? Remember many are in hospital. Has there been peace in your life this year? Have you come closer to God? Do you now know Him better? These are few of the achievements that some of us may take for granted. Your blessings does not always have to be in terms of how much you have in your bank account, whether you succeeded in getting a job, spouse or child within the year. You will still have them. God is never late. He is always on time. Remember, you can never run faster than God, so walk with Him in faith, obedience, service and constant fellowship. And you will be amazed to I see your numerous blessings. Shalom.

MAINTANING ALL
ROUND SUCCESS

The measure of success is not only about how much you have in your bank account or the position you occupy in the society. Therefore do not become sceptical at the mention of the word success here, because of your inability to meet your current financial demands. Success is all embracing; it could be financial as in your career, business advancement and of course the monetary gain. It could be physical, as in your good health. It could be spiritual, as in your level of relationship with God. In addition, it could be emotional, as in your relationship with your family and others. We can be successful in every aspects of life because it is the will of God for us to prosper and be in a good health. (III John: 2)

Been successful does not always have to do with money, even though it is the paramount bases for measuring success in today's world. A man who is considered very rich financially but unable to fully enjoy it due to constant ill health cannot really be said to be successful. Any success you have been able to achieved in any area of your life is worth cherishing and maintaining so that the enemy (Satan) would not take it away from you. For, we have been told that the three—fold work of the devil is to steal, kill and destroy (John 10: 10) There is the need therefore for you to know how to sustain your success so that your enemy does not steal it, destroy it or even attempt to kill you in the process. Failure to do so had drastically altered the fortune of so many people in the past. This should never be the portion of the children of God because He had promised us that we would be the head and not the tail, to be above, not beneath (Deut 28; 13)

The irony of it all is that apart from devious moves of Satan to change fortunes, some people have knowingly or unknowingly contributed to their downfall through their actions and omissions. It is very sad to see men and women who have reached the pinnacle of their careers to fall as a of their own making. Also, it is not palatable to witness a marriage that had lasted for so long fail due to the inability of the couple to resolve their differences. So how would you maintain that success you recorded so far in your life and how would you sustain the success you intend to achieve in the near future. One thing we all agree on is the need for us be successful, therefore here are some useful hints that we hope, will not only work for you but for others as you pass the message on.

PRAYERS

There is no undermining the essence of prayers in maintaining success in life. This is where many people miss it.It is very easy for us to constantly pray to God when we desire something but how many people bother to pray concerning the retention of whatever blessing God has given to them.The moment the blessing comes,a lot of people relax and concentrate more on enjoying what they have,forgetting that there is an enemy out there who is not happy with their success. "For we wrestle not against flesh and blood,but against principalities,against spiritual wickedness in high places.Wherefore take unto you the whole armour of God,that ye maybe able to withstand in the evil day,and having done all,to stand"(Eph6;12-13).A part of the armour here is prayer.And the Lord had already warned us that there will be evil days,which can come in the form of the trials and temptations we face.But in all,we have been consoled that we shall stand and not fall as we constantly use the armour(prayer) of God to defend ourselves and everything we possess.

Prayer is not just asking,it is also use for defence.Even in the physical world,anyone who leaves his door wide open at any time of the day would only have himself to blame when intruders comes in.Also in the spiritual,it is by consistence prayers that we can wage off the constant intruders that try to steal our joy,wealth,health,and everything that makes our lives meaningful.

You will be surprise to know the weight of spiritual physical attacks most successful people encounter on a daily basis. There have been cases of people finding fetish objects on their seats in offices,put there by those who are keen on removing them from there exalted position,even to the point of trying to kill them.Years ago,I listened to a testimony in a church of a man who narrated how he used to recite incantations and place fetish objects underneath the seat of the Managing Director, in the company where he was next in line to the Managing Director. His aim was to eliminate the man and take his place. There have been cases of people using various means to pull down their competitors.

In the same way, many homes and marriages that where once enjoying peace and unity are now in disarray due to the handiwork of evildoers.Some people that where once strong and healthy have become regular visitors to hospitals.This is why we must guide every area of our lives with constant prayers to God.No wonder the scripture tells us to pray without ceasing (1 Thess.5-19).We must endeavor to know God more in time of success,for it is He,who can help us to attain and sustain the success we already have.

DISCIPLINE

This is one word a lot of people are not comfortable with,but it is an invaluable asset you must have in order to attain and maintain success in life.(if you observe most successful people closely,you will discover a certain pattern of discipline in their lives).Even God disciplines us,His children (proverb.3;12). Indiscipline has led to the fall of many great men.

There are various levels of discipline.There is the physical disciplines,which involves your ability to continue to do those things that led to your present success.For instance,there have been cases of successful men and women suddenly exhibiting non-challant attitudes towards their jobs and businesses.They come to the office anytime they like,after all they are the boss. Some use the excuse of going for meetings or business trips to travel unnecessarily leaving the managing of the office in the hasnds of incompetent subordinates.Before they realize their mistake,their revenue begin to dwindle as a result of low productivity or even at times some unscrupulous staff use their habitual absence as an excuse to perpetuate fraud which is capable of grinding the company to a halt.If you read most interviews granted by top executives you would discover that most of them get to their office early and put in extra hours than their subordinates. Your physical discipline also involves your expenses.There is no need for you to show the world that you have "arrived" by acquiring the latest cars and the latest of every other thing. Use your resourses wisely so that your benefits will increase more and more (proverb 8;12).Mind you,there is nothing wrong in enjoying the wealth that God has given you, but instead of squandering it carelessly, you can channel it to the propagation of God's word by being a generous giver in your place of worship.

There is also the aspect of moral discipline. Immorality has led to the fall of many great men, even some men of God.

Some men see success as an avenue to acquire women and be seen with the most beautiful women around. They throw caution to the wind, forgetting their beautiful and dutiful wife and children at home and fall into the alms of strange women who are only in the relationship for material gains. No wonder the scripture says, that by means of a whorish woman, a man is brought to a piece of bread and the adulteress will hunt for the precious life.(proverb 6;26-27). Men of low moral character are easily distracted from their jobs, business,family, and gradually their success in these areas depreciate; and if care is not taken they loose out completely. Not so long ago, we all witnessed how a hard working president of one of the world's greatest country was almost ridiculed out of office due to his immoral relationship with a woman outside his marriage. His good works of many years was almost marred by that scandal. Even some men of God have been known to fall prey to the devices of the devil by allowing women to lure them to sin. The way out is discipline which is the ability to resist the devil and focus on the right things (James.4;7)

There is also the aspect of spiritual discipline which many successful people take for granted. Success is suppose to bring you closer to God and not to take you away from him, but there have cases where successful men and women become so pre-occupied with their jobs, business, family that they neglected the most important thing; constant fellowship with God and the brethren. They allow appointments to be fixed for the period they are suppose to be in church, gradually they even stop going to church completely. It is your responsibility to discipline yourself and set your priority right as regards time allocation to every sector of your life

HUMILITY

Many people had fallen from grace to grass as a result of lack of humility. They may have attributed their failure to other factors but the underlying factor was their immense pride. Success have been known to change some people from that of a humble and well-mannered person to that of a rude and arrogant individual who tends to look down on anyone perceived to be lesser in status. Some even carry their pride to church, expecting to be specially recognized by the church authority, and when they are not they move to another church. The word clearly tells in (Luke 18;14) that everyone who exalts himself will be humbled, and he who humbles himself will be exalted. Our greatest example of how to be humble comes from our Lord, Jesus Christ, who though being the son of God came down to earth as a man. He humbled himself and was obedient to the will of the father even unto death (Phil 2:6-8) If Jesus Christ did not count it demeaning to interact with mere mortals like us for thirty-three years on earth, how can a man suddenly feel too big to be seen with certain people because of the position he occupies in the society. Some people even snub their relatives and friends when they attain a position of importance. It is not necessary for you to help all of them as you can never satisfy everybody, but let it not be said that you deliberately ignored them or became rude to them when you can politely decline to assist when it is inevitable. Please show humility in your behavior at all times. Some people make a habit of boasting of their success to people not knowing who the enemy is amongst them. In the process they expose their secrets to their enemies who turn around to use such secrets against them. For instance a woman who has a loving and wonderful relationship with her husband does not have to constantly narrates all the "sweetness" to her neighbor when she is aware that the woman is currently having it rough in her own marriage. Instead she can show her neighbor that she cares by been there for her and offering useful advice when necessary. If you the type who always boast of your success, others will mock you at any little setback you encounter.

FOCUS:

No matter your level of success, you can still aim higher. Some people get so satisfied with their level of success that they become so complacent and before they realize it, their so called start diminishing instead of increasing. As long as we live we must continue to aim higher in our legitimate goals. Do not be static because you have gotten that big contract, life is never static. Even a President of a nation still need to plan how he can still remain relevant to the society after office. Your career, business, marriage, relationships must constantly be assessed and improved upon. We have been to told according to the scriptures not to be slothful in business, but to do it with the same fervency as we serve the Lord (Rom 12:11).

There is always room for improvement no matter you level of success. That your wonderful career, business, ministry still needs to be assessed regularly and improved upon. Lack of focus is responsible for the down turn of many business enterprises. They begin well by bringing out products acceptable to many people. Along the line, they refuse to inject new innovations into their products; before they realize what is happening rival companies have over-taken them in the lead and they are left in the lurch. Many companies have folded up as a result of lack of foresight. They fail to plan ahead and diversify when necessary in order to remain relevant in business world. A managing director who does not have a vision for his company would surely end up managing the company to a stand still. There is no doubt that we must remain focused in order to maintain whatever success we have achieved. Periodic assessment of our level of performance would help us to achieve more and do better, which is the hallmark of success.

CONTINUOUS LEARNING:

Leaning only ceases in the grave. Anyone who think that he has become too learned to learn more only set limitation for himself, and unfortunately what he had learnt may gradually become obsolete. Most successful people are great learners. They always seek to improve their knowledge and technical know-how. "Study to show thyself approved unto God, a work man that needed not be ashamed, rightly dividing the word of truth".(2 Tim.2;15)

Seek to improve yourself, your family, subordinates and all those who directly or indirectly contribute to your success.

INTERGRITY:

In today's world where there is so much cheating, lying and manipulations to get things done; the virtue of integrity has been relegated to the background. But no matter which way you see it, even if you get to the top by dubious means without integrity you will soon find yourself down again. No wonder the psalmist says "I have seen the wicked in great power, and spreading himself like a green bay tree, I sought him but he would not be found"(Ps 37:35-36)

Some top Executives of companies have been known to be bolted out of office for lack of integrity. They regard their position as an avenue to amass wealth at the expense of the growth of their organization. They used the opportunity given to them to enrich themselves, friends and those who assist them to perpetuate their fraudulent acts. Such prosperity is only for a short while. The moment the secret is out, that is the beginning of the end of their success.

It is a thing of pride to work meritoriously for years and retire peacefully. Such attitude does not only reflect on those involve but also on their children. This is why you see the children of certain individuals still being favored after the demise of their parents because of the great influence they had on others in the past; whereas some people are rebuff even when they are better qualified because of the bad reputation of their parents. No wonder, the bible says that "A good name is rather to be chosen than great riches, and loving favor rather than silver and gold."(Prov.22:1)

I was once at a workshop were the facilitators were mostly retired senior officers of the organization. Everything went quite well, until a particular man came to give a lecture, suddenly most of the participants became hostile and asked him very embarrassing questions which caused him visible discomfort. It turned out that the man was not only forced into early retirement, most of the staff who worked directly under him were dismissed as a result of forged documents he influenced them to sign. This man who had so much potential to climb to the top of his career was not only disgraced out of service but was still hated by all years later.

Even the fortunes of some churches have been known to decline due to the lack of integrity on the part of their leaders. In small scale ventures some people have devise means of cheating their their customers in order to make maximum profit. On the other hand, you find some shops are always busy attending to customers because they have been able to built a reputation of being honest and reliable. Therefore brethren, strive hard to retain your integrity, in the face of temptations. Your integrity will not only promote you but also sustain you all the way.

CRISIS MANAGEMENT

Finally, for you to be able to maintain that success you have been able to attain in any area of your life, be it financial, physical, spiritual, you must be a good crisis manager. Do not be naïve; no matter how successful you are today or how rosy your life seems to be, there will certainly be turbulent times. Some people clearly lack foresight or fail to acknowledge that there would still be hard times despite their current success. As a result they easily crumble when the problems come. This is why you see some couples who have enjoyed marital harmony for so long, suddenly going overboard when marital crisis arises. They quarrel unnecessarily, tell their problems to anyone who care to listen and at the end they magnify an otherwise simple marital dispute. It is the same in business settings, and even in the church, trying times are bound to come but our reaction at such times will determine whether the success so far attained is sustained or allowed to filter away. We should be able to identify and relate with people that have the required wisdom and knowledge to encourage us in times of need. Identify those who succeeded in whatever you are doing and seek their advice when necessary. For instance, in your career, you can have a mentor, someone you look up to, that can give you the necessary counsel when you need it Your pastor, trusted family members and friends can also assist you when necessary. However, your ultimate counselor is the Holy Spirit.

In addition, we must be able to know and do those things that will prevent major crisis from arising in our lives. Also make sure you employ the right people to help you in running your business.

In your relationships with your family, friends, colleagues, business partners and church members strive to understand one another note the particular differences in individuals.

Finally, remember it is not enough to work hard and achieve success; more importantly it is how you maintain it that matters. Occasionally you hear some people recounting the things they used to have; the number of cars, properties they owed; the position they once occupied; the peace they once enjoyed in their homes. This should not be the portion of children of God. Our covenant with God is to move from grace to grace, from glory to glory and from strength to strength in the mighty name of Jesus. Amen!

EXCESS BAGGAGE

Anyone familiar with the airport routine would know that there is a stipulated kilogram of load each passenger can carry on every trip. Any excess attracts penalty in form of payments or in some cases outright rejection of such luggage. In the same way, so many Christians are carrying excess load of sins, curses, bad habits, weighing them down thereby making a mockery of their salvation. "Thou shalt not have in thy bag divers' weights, a great and small" [Deut 25:13]. Why should you carry heavy burden of sins, curses, past mistakes when you have a God who is ever ready to take them away from you. He says, "Come unto me, all ye that labour and are heavy laden, and I will give you rest" [Matt 11: 28].

Brethren, being a born again Christian is not a status symbol, it is a serious business. You must be ready to wrestle with the enemy (Satan) through prayers, fasting in order to inherit the promises of God concerning you. Unfortunately, some Christians are like what I would describe as the "I Feel Alright" type of people. In my university days we used to call certain boys who resided in specific halls of residence; and as such regarded themselves as the best in the campus, as the 'I feel alright' guys. Even those amongst them who had neither looks nor brains still regarded themselves as the best in the campus as long as they reside in those halls. In a like manner, some Christians also have the same mentality, as long as they belong to a well known Pentecostal church, they feel all is well, forgetting that it is not the church that saves, but JESUS CHRIST himself. Being a member of a

Pentecostal church, being a worker in the church or even a Minister would not do much for you, if you are still caged in one way or the other by the strongholds of the enemy. Only you, know the areas in your life and that of your family that needs the special touch of God. At times, we just have to deal with our past for us to have a pleasurable today and tomorrow.

Were you a fornicator, adulterer, thief, murderer, plotter of evil etc before coming to Christ? Is there any pattern of problem in your family like bareness, poverty, sickness, and late marriages? Is there any problem in your life that seems to defy any solution no matter how hard you have tried? There may be need for you to seek for deliverance from the source of that problem. You may even be a Pastor and still not make much progress in life and ministry until you have undergone deliverance in certain areas of your life.

Unfortunately, the word deliverance has been completely removed from the vocabulary of some churches and in some cases, when it is mentioned; it is done derogatorily as if it is shameful to still be talking about deliverance after salvation. Brethren, do not be deceived, confessing salvation when you are fully aware that you have not totally renounced the past sins in your life, and you also have certain bad habits in your life that you have not been able to give up despite your level of Christianity will be the height of self-deception. Therefore deliverance is not only necessary; it is a must to obtain freedom from the kingdom of darkness.

Now let us examine some of the evil baggages that some Christians still carry, thereby hindering their overall progress in life.

BAGGAGE OF SIN

So many Christians have committed grievous sins in the past before giving their lives to Christ. Some are still deep in sins despite their new found faith, yet they delude themselves confessing that old things have passed away, whereas they have not fUlly confessed, renounced and repented of their sins. Beloved, sin is sin; there is no small or big sin. "Knowing this, that our old man is crucified with him that the body of sin might be destroyed that henceforth we should not serve sin" [Rom 6:6] if you are still battling with any sin and you are finding it difficult to let go, you need deliverance through fervent prayers, fasting or table the problem before the appropriate deliverance minister in your church for necessary action. Allow the word of God to work in your life "The spirit of the Lord is upon me because he hath anointed me to preach the gospel to the poor; he hath sent me to heal the broken hearted, to preach deliverance to the captives and recovering of sight to the blind to set at liberty them that are bruised" [Luke4:18.].

BAGGAGE OF CURSES;

Many Christians are still operating under curses, spells either self induced or inherited. As such, their lives are full of unexplainable trials and temptation. There is the need for thorough examination of your past and that of your family. You must not fold your arms when you are besieged by persistent problem that seem to defy every solution.

The reason that desired change has refused to come, could be as a result of certain curses operating in your life or family. Until such curses are broken and you are set free you cannot enjoy the fullness of your inheritance in Christ. That long standing bareness in your life despite, the fact that the doctors have certified you and your spouse healthy; that prolonged single status even though you have all the qualities to be a good wife/husband; that poverty that still lingers in spite of your hard work and determination; that long standing sickness that has plagued you for years, could be as a result of a curse or spell operating in your life or family.

How do curses come into people's life? It can come as a result of just being a member of a particular family because of the sins committed by your ancestors. For instance, Gehazi, the servant of Prophet Elisha had a curse placed on him and his generations when he deceived his master by receiving the money and gifts Elisha had earlier refused to collect from Naaman. II Kings 5:27. As such Gehazi had the leprosy of Naaman transferred to him and his generations.

This is why a serious Christian must dig into the past actions or misdeeds of his ancestors to ascertain if they have any correlation to their present predicament and be determined to have the yoke broken. Curses can also be invoked by words of mouth and actions. Some have stolen things or done evil in the past which had brought curses on them. Some parents have cursed their children in moments of anger being not aware of the repercussion later. Some people have even cursed themselves by their own words, all in the need to emphasis a point or prove their innocence. Be careful with what you say, the devil is always looking for what to use to ensnare the children of God. No wonder the Psalmist said, "I said I will take heed to my ways, that I sin not with my tongue, I will keep my mouth with a bridle, while the wicked is before me" [Ps. 39:1.]

BAGGAGE OF BAD HABBITS;

Bad Habits varies from one person to another. And if you are sincere with yourselves you would recognize the ones in your life; because it neither enhances your life nor your Christian race. Bad habits could include.

Laziness: In the family sector, there are many lazy husbands, wives, and children; always blaming others for anything that goes wrong whereas they are the ones not living up to their responsibilities. In the secular sector, there are many lazy workers, businessmen and women, always finding faults in others for their misfortune, instead of beaming the searchlight on themselves. Chances are that their lackadaisical attitude to work might be responsible for their stagnation and lack of progress and not their perceived enemies. In the church, some pastors, ministers, workers are lazy. They are not ready to put in the extra effort required for the physical and spiritual growth of the church.

Other examples of bad habits include: ¬Gossiping: spreading tales and creating disaffection all around.

Uncleanliness: Many people have lost wonderful opportunities in life as a result of their non-challant attitude to their physical appearance and their environment.

HOW TO GET DELIVERANCE:

Give your life to Christ: This is the first step. You must surrender completely to God. You must worship the Lord in truth and in spirit; not one leg in Christianity and the other out: If you are still involved in occultism and fetish practices by visiting herbalists, Spiritualists and questionable 'men of

God' for solution to your problem, then you have not fully surrendered your life to God. "Casting all your care upon him; for he careth for you" [I Peter 5:7] The key word here is all, not some; there is no problem, no situation, and no enemy that is greater than God. b) Use the word of God: The scripture says "that the word of God is God himself'. [John 1:1] Therefore it is impossible to get deliverance without the word of God. It is a pity that many Christians still do not take the word of God seriously. They are just contended with attending church service alone. Some do not even open the bible except in the church. Neither do they buy nor read other Christian literatures like books and magazines; yet they are still wondering why their lives have not changed significantly since they gave their lives to Christ. Brethren, what you do not have, you cannot use. If the word of God is not in you, it is not possible for you to use it to break the stronghold of the enemy in your life. Remember this, "for the word of God is quick and powerful, and sharper than any two edged sword, piercing even to the dividing asunder of soul and spirit and of the joints and marrow, and is a discerner of the thoughts and intents of the heart" [Heb 4:12.] Even the centurion soldier, who was not born again acknowledged the supremacy of the word of God when he said to Jesus "Lord I am not worthy that thou shouldest come under my roof, but speak the word only and my servant shall be healed" [Matt. 8:8].

C]. Use the blood of Jesus: The blood of Jesus is usually regarded as the last card. When all else seems to fail, use the blood of Jesus to combat that situation. Satan has no answer to it. This is why Pharaoh had no option but to let the children of Israel go after the Passover; when the Lord smote every first born of the Egyptian because they did not have the sign of the blood on their doorpost. "For the Lord will pass through to smite the Egyptians and when he seeth the blood upon the lintel and on the two side posts, the Lord will pass over the door, and will not suffer the destroyer to come into your houses to smite you"[Exod. 12:23]. If the blood of an earthly lamb could save the Israelites, you can imagine what the blood of the Son of God (the Lamb of God) can do for us.

Use it faithfully for total deliverance. Through the Holy Spirit:

The power of God through the Holy Spirit is used to deliver us from bondages. This is why so many people receive deliverance from various afflictions during church services, crusades when the move of the Holy Spirit is paramount. "The Spirit of the Lord God is upon me because the LORD hath anointed me to preach good tidings unto the weak, he hath sent me to bind up the broken¬hearted, to proclaim liberty to the captives, and the opening of the prison to them that are bound" [Isa. 61 :1]. Therefore there is no reason to be bound by the enemy when you have totally surrendered your life to Christ and you are filled with the Holy Spirit. But you must live a holy life for the spirit to dwell in you.

Where to go for deliverance;
This has become very important because of the existence of some churches and so called 'men of God' who use unscriptural methods to administer deliverance to gullible Christians; adding more to their problems.

(I)   Bible believing church: It is our duty as Christians to recognize and belong to a bible believing church, where the word of God is preached without addition or subtraction. There is nothing to be ashamed of when you realize that you need deliverance in certain aspects of your life. Approach your pastor or the deliverance Minister for necessary action to be taken. In many

Pentecostal churches, there is always a deliverance section on specific days and time of the week. Avail yourself of this opportunity when the need arises. You can also obtain your deliverance as you attend and partake in special church programmes, crusades organized for specific purposes.

(Ii)   Self-deliverance: This can be done when you genuinely purge yourself of evil acts. Jacob had to purge himself and his household of evil before he had his name changed from Jacob, the deceiver, usurper to Israel the Prince. "Then Jacob said unto his household and to all that were with him, put away the strange gods that are among you, and be clear, and change your garments" [Gen. 35:2].

Finally brethren, it is essential for us to know that deliverance is paramount for every Christian be you new or old in the faith. Any church that does not believe in it is not genuine. Bear in mind that, there is nothing to be ashamed of in seeking for deliverance. Do not allow the age or familiarity of the deliverance Minister to discourage you. If God has placed deliverance annointing on him/her utilize it to your advantage. In addition, know that deliverance is a continuous process as you faithfully walk with God, through fervent prayers, fellowship and constant study of the word of God. It is only a freeman that can move from one location to another, a man in the prison is limited. Therefore you must go the extra-mile to seek to be free from every limitation in your life. After all, "if the son therefore shall make you free, ye shall be free indeed" [In 8:36.]

You are free in Jesus name. AMEN

RELATIONSHIPS

'Relationships come in different kinds. There are relationships with one's family, with friends of both sexes, courtship between man and women, with colleagues at work, neighbors and even with fellow church members. Of all these types of relationship, it is only that with one's family that is binding on each and every one of us, because nobody 'can change the family they belong to. Moreover, God in his infinite wisdom has a purpose for making us a member of a particular family.

But we do have a say in our choice of friends, spouses and we can also determine to an extent, our level of association with our colleagues and neighbors. This is necessary because friendship with the wrong type of people have been known to cause a lot of havoc (Prov. 13 :20).

RELATIONSHIP WITH FRIENDS

We all need friends; good friends who will always be there for us when we need them, who will lift us up when we are down. Friends, who generally will enhance our spiritual, emotional and physical well being. Unfortunately, some friends have been known to affect people negatively to the extent that their destinies have been greatly altered. If you examine closely the confessions of most armed robbers, drug addicts and prostitutes in the society, you will discover that majority of them got into these destructive habits through wrong associations with some people in the disguise of friends. Today unless by God's mercy their lives maybe completely ruined.

This is why as Christians, we must be careful and prayerful in our choice of friends. You can be cordial in your attitude towards people without necessarily having most of them as close friends. It is imperative that you have friends whose lives and ways of life, have positive impact on you and draw you closer to God. Do not the mistake of keeping as close friends, people whose association with you will make you to depart from the ways of God. This is why Prov.27: 17 says that "Iron sharpeneth iron, so a man sharpeneth the countenance of his friend".

Our friends should be those who are able to counsel us with the Word and wisdom of God when we truly need them in that moment of discouragement; it is that friend who truly knows God that can uplift you. This is not to say that now that you have become a born-again child of God, you should completely forget your old friends who are yet to be saved. You can still affect their lives positively by constantly witnessing to them about our Lord Jesus Christ. But to still keep them as close friends and constant companies may lead to your spiritual and physical doom. It is time we realized that friendship is not by force but by choice. The bible records some men of God who had to separate from certain individuals before the purpose of God for their lives could be achieved. The case of Abraham readily comes to mind. God's promises to Abraham could not be fulfilled until he separated himself from Lot. Gen 13: 14-15, recorded that "the Lord said unto Abram, after Lot was separated from him, lift up now thine eyes and look from the place where thou are northward and southward, and eastward and westward. For all the land which thou seest, to thee will I give it and to thy seed forever". Maybe, the reason you have not had that breakthrough you have been waiting for all these years could be as a result of your refusal to separate yourself from those your worldly and ungodly friends. In this regard, one must be very careful and prayerful because you cannot really assess your relationship with friends on your own to know those that are good or not. The best way is to seek God's divine will. Ask the Lord to deliver you from wrong associations by causing a clean separation between you and them and by allowing them go the opposite direction from you.

RELATIONSHIP BETWEEN MAN AND WOMAN (COURTSHIP)

In the quest for love and life partners, many young men and women have been deceived and even had their destinies changed by their involvement with some so-called eligible bachelors and spinsters. This is why marriageable brothers and sisters need to be very careful and prayerful in their choice of life partners. The time of courtship or search for a spouse is always prone to temptations that if care is not taken some are led astray and may even loose their salvation. Some young men go into several relationships knowing fully well that they are not ready to be committed to anyone. Some already have a stereotyped copy of their kind of woman in mind. This makes choice of relationships to be judged purely on physical appearance, educational background, the kind of job a lady/ man has or his/her family background. There is nothing wrong in knowing what you desire in a woman, but the best way is to have an open mind and ask God to lead you to your spouse, the very bone of your bone, flesh of your flesh (Gen. 2:23). Do not be deceived by outward appearance or how religious a brother/ sister is. Remember we only see what is outside but God sees and knows everything.

AGREE WITH GOD

Do you really agree with the word of God as contained in the Holy Bible? Or are you like many Christians who take delight in disputing, debating and analyzing the word of God to suit their own situations and human understanding?
Please pause here, and examine yourself.

In this end time, there is so much controversy surrounding the word of God particularly among some men of God. This is understandable, considering the fact that Jesus Christ himself had told us (Matt: 24: 11) that in the last days many false prophets shall rise and shall deceive many. Many Christians are in absurd debates, concerning the issue of paying tithe and other salient commands given to us in the scriptures by God.

We are not to be swayed by the strange views of these so-called men of God who parade themselves as angels of light, using such controversial issues as a publicity stunt to advertise themselves and their church, Rather we are to focus our eyes and mind on what God himself has spoken for example concerning tithe: In Mal. 3: 10-12, written, "Bring ye all the tithes into the store house, that there may be meat in mine house, and prove me now herewith, saith the LORD of hosts. If I will not open you the windows of heaven and pour you out a blessing, that there shall not be room enough to receive it. And I will rebuke the devourer for your sakes, and he shall not destroy the fruits of your ground; neither shall your vine cast her fruit before the time in the field, saith the

59

LORD of hosts. And all nations shall call you blessed: for ye shall be delightsome land, saith the Lord of hots."

Nobody can add or subtract from the word of God. And God will not break his covenant nor alter His word (psalm 89:34). Your duty as a Christian is to believe and obey and you will receive your reward. Nobody can claim to know more than their maker "There is no wisdom nor understanding nor counsel against the LORD" Prov. 30. It is fruitless for anyone to try to add, substract or dilute the word of God by his own human understanding. It is only the Holy Spirit that can give us the true meaning of whatever God has hidden in His word. And the Bible has been written in such a simple way for any born again, spirit filled believer to read and Understand, A faithful tither will always have testimonies of God's faithfulness, no matter the economic situation you can never fault God. He has told us of what He would do for us when we pay our tithes regularly, and we can be sure of his faithfulness.

Your own part is to agree with Him by obeying Him and you will see the result. You must understand that God cannot lie. A survey of churches have shown that, the spiritual {and physically vibrant ones are those who strictly adhere to God's commands. After all, God is a rewarder of them that diligently seek him (Heb. 11 :6) What many Christians fail to realize is that their groans and travails concerning their financial life is as a result of their disobedience. If you are not been faithful with the little you have today, it means you will certainly not be faithful if given more.

Therefore, my beloved brethren do not let anyone deceive you with strange interpretation of the word of God as contained in the scriptures. The scriptures has been for centuries, ever before we were born and it shall remain forever for our Lord

Jesus had said "Heaven and earth shall pass away: but my words shall not pass away" Luke 21:33

GOD'S WORD CONCERNING YOUR LIFE AND SITUATION

Even when God speaks to us directly or through men of God concerning our lives and situations, at times we still deliberately refuse to agree with Him just because the pronouncement does not conform to our prayers and expectations. Take the case of a born again sister who has been asking God for a life partner for years. Inwardly, her expectation is to have a handsome and rich husband, but alas! a young, average looking brother with few possessions approaches her for marriage. And after prayers and communion with God she is told by God to go ahead and marry the man. Instead of thanking God for this gift she uses her human intelligence to distort the fact and refused to marry the man. Meanwhile her eyes may be on a young handsome rich brother whom she erroneously believe is the man for her. To buttress her point, she even quotes the bible passage which says that "Every good gift and every perfect gift is from above, and cometh down from the Father of lights, with whom is no varableness, neither shadow of turning" James 1;17 The truth is that what seems perfect today may actually turn out to be the exact opposite. Whereas that young man who does not seem to meet the sister's expectation today may turn out to be a great blessing later.

Today, many young Christian brothers and sisters are roaming the streets looking for jobs; some with very good qualifications. It is possible that God had been ministering to some of these people about a particular business so as to be established, even though the job may seem less prestigious.

Instead they are looking for non-existent white collar jobs or trying to raise huge sum of money to start a big business. At the end, there may be so much frustration in their lives that they even contemplate leaving the church and doing what unbelievers do to succeed, such as stealing. The solution may be that your job is just been delayed so that God will give you the very best or that you have refused to yield to the leading of the Holy Spirit who had been telling you to start that small scale business in your house. There is nothing wrong in making potato or plantain chips for sales in school, offices or any other services which ordinarily you may have regarded as beneath your standard. You will be surprised how a humble beginning can result into something great as long as it is the will of God. What about you my dear sister in Christ who has been married for years without the fruit of the womb. All the doctors have told you that you and your husband are alright and you have been assured by the word of God that in due time you will surely know the joy of motherhood Instead of agreeing with the word of God which says 'Lo children are an heritage of the LORD: and the fruit of the womb is his reward "Psalm 127:3 you run from one church to another, from one herbalist to another seeking for what God says is your heritage.

The list is endless of how in our individual lives we have stubbornly refused to obey God's word concerning our lives and situations, which had always resulted in frustrations in our walk with God.

So what is it that God has said in the scriptures or spoken concerning your situation in life that you have not been able to totally agree with and obey? Save yourself from necessary anxiety and frustration by agreeing totally with God no matter how unpalatable it may seems to you today. You can be sure, that the glory of the Lord will certainly be revealed at the right time. After all there is no searching of his understanding (Isaiah 40:28). No amount of controversy will change the word of God, whether it is written in the Bible. or it has been revealed directly to you. Abraham is today regarded as the Father of many nations because of his obedience to God.

Even when he was told by God to offer his only son Isaac as a burn offering unto the Lord, he did not argue with God or tried to wriggle out of it by pretending that he did not hear from God as many of us would have done. For this reason, he received all that God had promised him.

Finally, let each one of us strive to be in agreement with God by believing the scriptures, obeying God's word in totality This will make our faith walk a lot easier and we shall receive all the wonderful benefits of God has reserve for his children, make up your mind now to agree totally with God. Ask the Lord to give you the spirit of obedience and understanding and you will surely receive in Jesus name. Amen.

COURAGE TO SAY NO

"I cannot take it anymore. I am out of this marriage" says Agnes! "Come on", replied her good friend Joy, "you cannot opt out now, marriage IS tor life". "Why did you marry him in the first place'? It is obvious the two of you are not compatible" says an older colleague who had been listening to the conversation of the two friends. With a restrained voice. Agnes replied, "my sister! What could I have done, there I was at 35, still single; family and societal pressure was mounting on me to settle down, so when he came along I said yes to his proposal even though I knew he was-not a born-again Christian. Moreover, he had the support of my family-and I did not have the courage to say no to him at that age".

Does the above story sound familiar? Many have gone through similar experience and others might currently be passing through the same. but the difference is that they had the courage and boldness to say no instead of mortgaging their happiness like Agnes. After all the Bible had made it clear to us that we will all face trials. "There hath temptation taken you but such as is common to man but ho will not suffer you to be tempted, above that ye are able but will with the temptation also make a way to escape, that ye may be able to bear it" I Cor 10.13. Your ability to manage these trials will determine whether you end up a victor or a victim.

Many lives have been ruined because those involved refuses to say no at the right time. Daily, school children, teenagers, adults are recruited into the evil world of smoking. alcoholism, cultism.

prostitution. armed robbery, corruption and other such vices, and many of them do not realize their foolishness until it is too late.

It is bad enough to be ignorant of certain issues. but even worse to know the truth and still go ahead to disobey. "And ye shall know the truth and the truth shall make you (John 8:32) From observation, ceetain reasons can be deduced at to why some people find it difficult to say no even when it is most appropriate. Some of these reasons are explored below:

1. The desire to please others:

Are you a man pleaser? Someone who always wants to do what others expect of him even when it is wrong. Then you have a problem because situations would arise when you are forced to say 'yes' instead of 'no' just to be accepted by those you aim to please. Brethren, remember you can never satisfy everybody. It is foolhardy to please men and displease God and yourself. You must have the courage and courtesy to say no at the right time even to those you hold in high esteem, when you are convinced it is the right thing to do. Shadrach, Meshach and Abednego refused to worship the golden image that Nebuchadnezzar made at the expense of their lives. They were not only rescued from their enemies but were promoted (Dan. 3). So also did Daniel ignored the evil decree that he should not pray to God in order to please the king. The Lord did not only rescue him from the mouth of the lions, he prospered during the reign of the same king who made the decree. Dan 6:20-28.

2. The need to belong:

It is everyone's desire to be loved and accepted where we find ourselves be it in school, office, market, church. Nevertheless, as children of God we must have our own guiding principle which must be in line with the word of. As such, you must never join others in doing wrong just to be accepted by them. Peer group pressure has led many young people in school, higher institutions of learning into occultism, drugs, prostitution and the inherent problems associated with such. Some people have become jobless because they connived with others to defraud their employers. Many people in government are now corrupt because they see others doing the same and do not want to be seen as fools who do not know how to become rich. "Be not thou envious against evil men, neither desire to be with them" Provo 24: 1.

3. GREED;

Many people find it difficult to say no especially when it comes to the issue of money. And the devil capitalizes on this to introduce demonic proposal to them "For the love of money is the root of all evil, which some converted after, they have erred from the faith, and pierced themselves through with many sorrows" I Timothy 6: I o. Are you greedy? Check yourself

4. Finally some people cannot say no when it matters most, not because they do not want to, but because they are just naturally weak-minded and fearful. This should not be the situation with any child of God. Christianity is synonymous with boldness and courage. "For God hath not given us the spirit of fear: but of power, and of love, and of a sound mind" II Tim. 1 :7. If you are still easily afraid of your fellow man, revisit the foundation of your Christianity; re-dedicate your life to God, yield yourself completely to God. He would strengthen you and give you a renewed mind and spirit.

A.   Say No To The Devil:

Every child of God must be ready to consistently say no to the various temptations that the enemy brings our way. Have you ever wondered why a man would take the life of his fellow man just to get wealth? And when he is caught he blames it on the devil and poverty whereas there are still many so-called poor people all over the world who have not taken to doing evil just to survive. The truth is that it is the devil that plants such evil thought in their heart and imagination. Instead of them to resist the devil by casting it out from their heart, they fertilize it by dwelling on it, imagining it and eventually committing the crime. No wonder the scripture says "submit yourselves therefore to God, resist the devil and he will flee from you" James 4:7.

Your resistance must be consistent because the enemy is very persistent. Do not say no today and compromise tomorrow. There is nothing to gain from doing wrong to advance in life; because ultimately you will still loose it all. When the devil gives with one hand, he uses the other to take two away from you. Do not compromise with the enemy, no matter how profitable the venture seems to be. Say no to all the evil thoughts and imagination he brings to your heart and no to the various temptations that daily besiege the children of God. Remember even Christ was tempted by the devil (Mark 1: 13) and He did not fall. There should never be an agreement between a child of God and the devil, therefore even before he ask, the answer should be No.

B.   Say No To Immorality

Immorality is gradually becoming a cankerworm eating deep into the society. The virtue of morality has been relegated to the background more so in these days of advanced technology where even children have access to the internet, pornographic films, provocative movies and magazines. Nowadays, even the so-called fashion of some youth says a lot of the moral decadence in the society. Sexual harassment has become a norm in the higher institutions and even in the corporate world. Some students even harasses the teachers sexually in exchange for good grades in their exams instead of studying to pass. Some ladies who are not ready to defile themselves find it difficult getting good jobs or promotions in their place of work while others actually use their sensuality to advance their career, believing it is their only way forward. Who are they fooling? Many women have excelled and are still excelling in various fields of endeavor without resulting to debasing their womanhood. Do not be attracted to the vain promises of men, work hard, know your God ultimately and you will reach the top. This is what the scripture says concerning immorality, "Marriage is honorable in all, and the bed undefiled; but whore mongers and adulterers God will judge "Heb.13:4.

C. Say No to Corruption

Corruption has almost become a norm in the society. Nowadays anyone in a position of power that refuses to corruptly enriched himself is seen as stupid by his friends and even the family. Corruption can be found from the bottom of the ladder to the very top, even children of God are not left out. But this is clearly contrary to what God says in the scriptures and anyone involved is disobeying God. "Thou shall not defraud thy neighbor, neither rub him: the wages of him that is hired shall not abide with thee all night until morning" Lev. 19: 13. But today what do you see? Many workers are wallowing in poverty while their employers are eating fat and trading with their wages. As children of God, we must abhor corruption in every form even when you are in the midst of the most corrupt. You must show good example and refuse to be lured into their evil dealings. It does not matter if they mock or even persecute you, as long as you do not yield to their negative demand God will stand by you and you will be vindicated. "If ye be reproached for the name of Christ, happy are ye; for the Spirit of glory and of God resteth upon you: on their part he is evil spoken of, but on your part he is glorified". 1 Peter4: 14.

D. Say No To Bad Friends

Finally, we—are hereby encouraged to say no to bad friends. This may not be easy but it is something that has to be done for us to achieve our goals. After all, friendship is not by force but by choice. When you observe that your friendship with someone or a group has become the devil's point of contact for leading you astray, then you must break away from such friends no matter how long it has been. After all, friends are suppose to add value to your life and not to devalue it "Ointment and perfume rejoice the heart: so doth the sweetness of a man's friend by hearty counsel" Prov. 27:9. Brethren, be wise, do not allow the evil counsel of a friend to ruin your life. Say No to bad friends today. You do not need them, you have Christ, your true friend. Shalom!

FREEDOM AT LAST

Freedom from what! Someone might ask. Well, it could be from anything, whatever you want to be free from. It could be those so-called little vices in your life you have been trying to give up—lying, cheating, back-biting, laziness. More importantly, we are referring to that burden, problem or reproach that has plagued your life for so long, that it causes you to almost doubt your salvation.

Ask that woman who has just given birth to a baby after ten years of waiting on the Lord, and she would gladly tell you what it means to be free from the reproach of 'barrenness'. Ask that man or woman who has been healed of a long-standing disease; ask the man who has just gotten a good job after seven years of graduation from the university and he would gladly declare to you the true meaning of 'freedom'. Freedom from every affliction is our 'covenant' right as children of God because, He had promised us, that even though we would have afflictions, He would deliver us from them all (psalm 34:19)

In reality, freedom (that is, what it means) is peculiar to individuals. The problem you may be anxious to get rid of in your life could be entirely different from mine. As our faces differ, so does our problems and circumstances. There is no one alive who does not have a need of one thing or the other from God.

There is no perfection in anyone but God hence, if you think you have anything to be free from, ask the Lord who knows how to take away those things in your life that does not glorify His name. "The Lord will perfect that which concerneth me; thy mercy o Lord, endureth'. forever, forsake not the works of thine own hands". (Psalm 138 :8)

It is a pity that there are still many people, even born again Christians who are not aware that they are still in a cage, one way or another. Some have come to see their faults as one of those things that would just go away. Deceiving people, telling lies is not regarded as a problem to them as long as they can get away with it. Beware, one day you will be caught in your own web of lies and deception. Some people regard certain trials in their lives as a family problem; therefore they have become complacent allowing the devil to deal with them unnecessarily. Who told you, you must suffer from a particular illness because those before you on suffered the same disease? And for you to say that since the women in your family always have miscarriages, then it would be your portion too? Remember that at as a result of your new birth in Christ, you now belong to the superior family of our Lord. Bear in mind that the scripture says "Surely he hath borne our grieves and carried our sorrows: yet we did esteem him stricken, smitten of God and afflicted. But he was wounded for our transgressions, he was bruised for our, iniquities; the chastisement of our peace was upon him and with his stripes we are healed" (Is 53:4-5).

Two incidents happened the same day that the Holy Spirit used it to inspire me to write this article. In the morning, I saw a man I had not seen for a long time, a 'family man' whom everyone has come to recognize as a drunkard. To my dismay, he was still the same, despite repeated efforts by many people to counsel him and preach to him as well as leading him to the church. To this particular man, the pressing need was to be free from the spirit of drunkenness'.

That same day, in the evening, I came across a junior colleague in my establishment who I had cause to counsel a year earlier, concerning his drinking habit which had resulted in some health problems. And to my pleasant surprise, this man had changed completely for the better; instead of the usual red eyes and agitated movements, he was calm, fresh and healthy. All he could talk about was how God had saved him from drinking alcohol and that today, he detests the sight of it not to talk of tasting it. In fact, he had parted ways with his erstwhile drinking partners. To this man, his freedom has come and a great transformation has taken place in his life. Just as the Lord transformed (the life of Jacob, the deceiver to 'Israel'—the 'prince' (Gen 32:8). In the same way, he transformed the life of Saul the persecutor of the church to (Paul) one of the greatest apostles (Acts 9:1-6).

Also Hannah, the barren woman (scorned by her enemy) became the mother of a great prophet, 1 Samuel 1:19-20). Our God is still the same, and He can do it for any of His children who earnestly desire a good change in his\her life.

WHY DO WE NEED TO BE FREE?

The need for us to be free from afflictions in our lives cannot be over-emphasized. A visit to the prison yards (and to the inmates therein) would make you cherish the freedom of movement you take for granted everyday. So much more, we would appreciate the need to be free from all the physical, emotional, spiritual and, financial problems that besets the world we are in.

First, you must identify your own problem and be determined to put an end to it. "And ye shall know the truth, and the truth shall make you free" (John 8:32).

We need to be free from every affliction of life so that our testimonies will glorify the name of the Lord. To be realistic, no matter how committed you are as a Christian, so long as there is a visible reproach in your life, doubts may be cast in the minds of those doubting 'Thomases' of the world when you witness to them concerning the goodness of God.

Two years ago, a lady I know so well narrated to me, how some colleagues in the office were always mocking her because she was always cheerful and constantly preaching to them to give their lives to Christ; whereas she had been married for seven years without bearing children. Today, she is a proud mother of a set of twins (a boy and a girl) and those same colleagues who once mocked her now sing her praise. As a mater of fact, some of them gave their lives to Christ as a result of her testimony, Brethren, let us not seat back and allow the enemy (the devil) to steal the wonderful blessings (John 10:10) that God has promised us. We must rise up and shine so that the world will see the glory of God in us even before we open our mouths to preach to them.

Secondly, it is often said that 'experience is the best teacher' therefore, your personal experience in any area of your life would enhance your knowledge and confidence to counsel and teach others in similar situations when necessary. It is that man who has been able to overcome poverty that can boldly tell the poor that Christianity is not synonymous with poverty, because the silver and gold of this world belongs to our 'Father' (Haggai 2:8). Do not get me wrong, I am not saying that you cannot help others in areas where you need help yourself; all I'm saying is that it would be easier for you to have mastered a situation before you can be seen to be an authority on that issue. This is why it is not the best that the marriage counselors should be the 'singles' in the church.

KEYS TO FREEDOM

1. Give your life to Christ Complete surrender of oneself to God is the basic pre-requisite for freedom from the various yokes satan puts on the peoples of this world. Rom 10:13 says that "for whosoever shall call upon the name of the Lord shall be saved". You must first of all, come to God (yourself with all that you have before you can even contemplate freedom. It is not a partial surrender, where today, you are in one church, and tomorrow you are visiting one 'spiritualist' looking for solutions to your problems. Those who put their trust in men or any other power, apart from God's power will always be disappointed. "Thus saith the Lord: cursed be the man that trusteth in man and maketh flesh his arm, and whose heart departeth from the Lord" "Blessed is the man that trusteth in the Lord and whose hope the Lord is" (Jer. 17:5,7).

2.   Persistent prayers

Brethren, if you cannot pray fervently do not expect an early freedom from your afflictions. The enemy is very subtle, at times it may seems that a trial is over, only for it to re-surface with more intensity. And if you are the type with a casual attitude towards prayers, your strength will give you away and you will become overwhelmed by the situation, No wonder we are told to pray without ceasing. (1 Thess 5:17). Prayer is not a once-a-while or twice a day thing. It is a continuous exercise as the Holy Spirit leads you. It could be at home, office, shop, car even on the on the road. Do not allow inconvenience to deprive you from praying.

There is a danger in waiting for a convenient place and time to pray even, when we have a burden to pray. The enemy can use the time lapse before you get to 'convenient' place to cause havoc. There is no restriction to where and how long you can pray until you obtain the desired result (1 john 5 :14-15).

3.   Positive Attitude and Confession

It is amazing to see how some people behave and say negative things concerning their lives, family and even the country and still expect the best. What we say is heard by both God and the enemy. While God is bound by his word to confirm that which we say to his ears, but because he is a merciful father, he can always forgive us for our negative confessions; but the enemy on the hand uses it to accuse us before the throne of God. Therefore we must be very careful what we say about ourselves.' "For with the heart, man beliveth unto righteousness and with the mouth, confession is made unto salvation" (Rom10:10). Even though, many people believe thy are capable of accomplishing certain things in their lives, they are afraid to voice it out because they do not want others to laugh at them. Joseph told his brothers his dreams, they did not only mock him, they also persecuted him (Gen 37:5-9) but at the end, it came to pass. Out of the twelve spies sent to spy the land of Canaan, only Joshua and Caleb brought positive reports concerning the ability of Israel to posses the promised land (Joshua 14:6-7). Little wonder it was only the two of them (out of all the spies and those who accompanied them) eventually entered the Promised Land. What you' cannot say, do not expect to have. No matter your current situation, see your freedom from it, say it and possess it.

4.   Tenacity

The dictionary defines being tenacious as follows; to hold tightly, refusing to let go". What is it that God has promised to do for you and you are almost tired of waiting? You have prayed, fasted still trusting the Lord and yet, no results. Hold on still, refuse to give up. Do not allow any temptations to discourage you from doing good works, as is the case with some people. They get tired of waiting for God to solve a particular problem for them and, they erroneously turn back to solve the problem the worldly way.

And the result usually, is that they find themselves in a worse state than before. Bear in mind that endurance is part of your inheritance in Christ. If Jesus did not endure the shame on the cross, where would we be today? Therefore, my beloved, be steadfast, unmovable, always abounding in the work of the Lord, for as ye know that your labor is not in vain in the Lord" (1 Cor 15:58).

Even at the last minute, God will still show up. At times, he purposely allows us to endure until we are almost giving up, to show Himself strong in our situation. But remember, He will never allow us to go through a temptation that we cannot bear (1 Cor 10:13). He will always make a way for us to escape out of every bad situation. That your future that seems so bleak right now will surely, be better. That your business that has refused to improve will surely grow. That your spouse, or child that has. refused to come will certainly become reality. Whatever it is that you desire, you will get it as long as you put complete trust in the Lord. Pray and be obedient to His word.
Finally, your freedom from affliction glorifies the name of the Lord. We were not created for problems and reproaches, we were created to have dominion on earth and to be perfect

like our father (Gen 1 :26). Whatever is contrary to God's will in your life has to go. The Lord does not delight in seeing us suffer. He says that His thought towards us are good and not evil (Jer. 29:11). It is up to you to recognize your problem and earnestly desire to be free from it.

Work towards your miracle with prayers, commitment to the work of God and obedience to His word. Then you must be ready to endure until your freedom comes. After all, the blood of Jesus already obtained our total liberty. You are free in Jesus name. AMEN.

WHY WORRY?

Why not? You may say, after all, there is so much to worry about. Yes, we all know that life is full of 'ups and downs' and that currently, you may be going through difficult situations, but have you ever paused to ask yourself what benefits worrying over those situations have brought to your life? The truth remains that worrying never solves any problem instead it compounds it. Little wonder the Lord spoke on the need for us not to worry about our lives, what to eat, drink or wear but to seek the kingdom of God first, and all that we need will be added unto us *(Matt 6: 19-33)*. He went further to say, " . . . *take therefore no thought for the morrow, for the morrow shall take thought for the things of itself, sufficient unto the day is the evil thereof'* (Matt 6: 34).

Mind you, we do acknowledge the fact that there is no human being that is totally immune to 'worrying'; however it is the extent to which you worry and your attitude towards it, that will determine the effects it would have on your life. We acknowledge the fact that there are various reasons that may lead to worrying, however, we will examine the commonest or most prevalent causes.

POVERTY

There is no doubt that poverty is a source of worry to many people particularly, in the face of the economic situations in the country. A lot of people are struggling to meet the basic necessities of life. Joblessness is on the increase and many businesses are not progressing. But even in the midst of all these, many people are still prospering. Most wealthy people we see today were not born into rich families; you would be surprised at the humble beginning of most of them, and how they had to strive to get to their present position. It was not by worrying about their poor background. In most cases, you would discover that hard work; faith in God and determination to succeed were propelling factors behind their success. *"If ye be willing and obedient ye shall eat the good of the land"* (Isaiah 1: 19). You must be ready to put God first in your life and obey him and He will lead you to success. Many people allow anxiety to becloud their reasoning such that even when God is giving them insight into a productive venture, they are unable to see. They struggle unnecessarily on their own relying on their own ability and on the goodwill of family and friends to get out of their financial predicament forgetting that it is written in the scriptures that; *"The silver is mine, and the gold is mine saith the Lord of hosts"* (Haggai 2:9). Put your trust in the Lord who owns what you need <u>serve him faithfully and</u> you will have your heart's desire. But if you put your trust only on 'human connections' relatives and contracts, at the end, you may be disappointed. *"Cursed be the man that trustheth in god and maketh flesh his arm and whose heart departeth from the Lord (Jer 17:5)* and *"Blessed is the man that trusteth in the Lord, and whose hope the Lord is"* (Jer 17:7).

If you have been disappointed because someone whom you expected to help you out of your poor financial predicament turned you down, put your trust in God. He can use anyone to help you even those who have said 'no' to you before. This is why you must not give in to anxiety because an anxious mind cannot serve God faithfully. Allow God to lead you, do not harden your heart when you are being led to start that small-scale business instead of the big corporate job you desire. Most big companies and organizations you see today, started small. And if your current job is not meeting your needs, do not despair; continue to put in your best as you look for a better job. Do not wait until you have that fantastic job before putting in your best. Remember what the scripture says, *"Whatsoever thy hand findeth to do, do it with thy might..." (Eccl9: 10)*. When the Lord sees your commitment in little things, He always sets you up for greater ones.

HEALTH PROBLEMS

This also creates a lot of anxiety in the lives of people. For some individuals any minor sickness puts the fear of death in their hearts. If you are in the category of those relatively more prone to ill health, do not worry, you will not die but live to declare the wonderful works of God in your life *(Psalm 118: 17)*. So, the fear of dying from that sickness should not come into your mind. The price for that sickness was paid for you more than two thousand years ago when our Lord Jesus shed His blood on the cross of Calvary. This is why the scripture says " ... *surely he had borne our grief and carried our sorrows... and with his stripes we are healed (Isaiah 53: 4-5)*. Most of the miracles Jesus performed while on earth was on healing, and these miracles are still manifesting today in the lives of many therefore do not allow anxiety to 'make you believe a lie of the devil.

In addition, avoid things that may bring sickness such as over-eating and drinking, over-working yourself and uncleanliness. Have it in your sub consciousness' always that your body is the temple of the Spirit of God. And where light is, darkness (sickness) must disappear. And if your anxiety still persists, bring the situation before servants of God in the church, many of whom God has been using to set many free from the bondage of sickness. *"Is any sick among you? Let him call for the elders of the church and let them pray over him, anointing him with oil in the name of the Lord"* (James 5:14).

LATE MARRIAGE

This issue of late marriage has gradually become a problem in our society over the years. This can be attributed to the fact that many more people particularly, young men and women, are getting more educated (which takes time) and as well, becoming more aware of the importance of having the right partner in order to have a successful marriage. The innate desire to find the right partner has become a source of worry, particularly to the children of God ('believers') who sometimes experience delays in this 'area', despite their commitment to God. To compound the problem, the 'society' and 'families' do not help matters by their constant harassment of these perceived 'eligible' spinsters and bachelors on the need for them to change status 'marital-wise'. This has resulted in many young men and women worrying themselves to the point of making 'irreparable' mistakes in their lives.

People that are constantly nursing 'worry' in their hearts end up falling victims in this area. Anxiety will lead you into wrong hands because Satan delights to use is at a ready trap. It is when you are desperate to marry that Satan would bring his own candidate to you. But on the other hand, if you relax and let God have his way, he would give you the best spouse. Remember, *"Every good gift and every perfect gift cometh down from heaven and from the Father of lights with whom there is no variableness nor shadow of turning"* (James 1: 17).

It is up to you; if you just want to satisfy societal expectations (and your desire) and 'jump' into marriage with the next man or woman that comes your way or you want the Lord to give you 'the bone of your bones' and 'the flesh of your flesh' (*Genesis* 2:23) you must be 'still' and allow God to exalt His name in your situation. Stop comparing yourself with others. Your own time will come. Meanwhile, strive to excel in other areas of your life spiritual, academics, career or business while waiting for your 'Mr. right' or 'Miss right', so that when it eventually happens, you would be a blessing to the family.

FAMILY PROBLEMS

This comes in various dimensions.

Many people are constantly worrying about one problem or the other in their family. These could vary from issues having to do with 'the children', 'the husband', 'the wife', 'in-laws', money. Some have become so used to worrying that when some 'gladdening' things happen in the family, they still refuse to celebrate and instead, they dwell on the minor issues that are yet to be resolved or settled. When the children bring home good 'reports' (results) from school at the end often, instead of being thankful to God, they would busy themselves with worrying where the next term's school-fees would come from. For the young couples that are yet to have children, the anxiety could even be more. It is general knowledge that the normal expectation after marriage is for children to follow; unfortunately, this is not always the case with some people. And instead of love and understanding from family and society, at times the couple especially, the woman gets unnecessary pressure and harassment particularly, from in-laws.

If you find yourself being confronted with this kind of situation, know that many people have passed through the same situation and overcome, therefore, you are not the first and certainly, not be the last. 1.cor 10: 13 says, *"There hath no temptation taken you but such as is common to man, but God is faithful who will not suffer you to be tempted above ye are able, but will with the temptation also make a way of escape, that ye may be able to bear it"*. Also bear in mind that it is God that gives children, not man or man-made gods, therefore, do not compound your problems by moving from one place to another in search of a solution, it will only lead to more frustration.

A. <u>FAMILY FINANCE</u>: This is another source of worry to many people. The desire to take proper care of the family is normal but if all you do is constantly worry, about how to get more money for family use, you would soon become a problem to the family. Undue comparison with other families that is, how well they are doing, often leads to depression, envy and at times, desperation sets in. Some men are so prone to money related anxiety that even when they have money, they cannot relax until they have more and it becomes a vicious circle. Bear in mind that though, money can get you most of your needs, it is not the solution to all of your problems. Instead of worrying, get connected to the source of 'true' wealth, for the scriptures say, *"But my God shall supply all your need according to his riches in glory by Christ Jesus"* (Phil 4:19). And remain committed to the things of God as you work hard to improve your condition of life. It is never late.

b. Persecution from <u>relatives</u>: Family 'squabbles' is also a cause of anxiety to so many people. It is a fact that some people are constantly depressed in their homes as a result of persecution from their spouses, in-laws, parents and even neighbors. The desire of some born-again children of God to commit more time and talent to the service of God has met with stiff resistance from their family members. Do not allow this negative behavior to wear you down. The Lord had foreknowledge of this, which is why he said, *"Ye and all that will live godly in Christ shall suffer persecution"* (2 Timothy 3: 12). He also promised us that *'in all these things, we are more than conquerors through him that loved us'* (Rom 8:37).

PHYSICAL APPEARANCE

Some people are so concerned about their looks that it has become a great source of worry in their lives. This is particularly common with the womenfolk; it is either they believe they are too fat, too slim, too dark, too fair or ugly as the case may be. If you consider this problem, instead of brooding about it, do something positive. Exercise regularly; eat healthy diet and loose weight (or add weight as the case may be). Brighten up your appearance by strictly adhering to clean personal hygiene, and above all, smile. A smile goes a long way to make you look attractive. Remember, nobody was created ugly. We were all created in the image of God (Gen 1:27).

Has someone told you that you are ugly? Instead of worrying about it, look at yourself in the mirror and declare that 'you are fearfully and wonderfully made by God'. Discover your good attributes and enhance them. Also, look out for your flaws (could be your skin, dressing, carriage) and work on it for improvement. Above all, do not allow negative comments to pull you down. Know that God did not create you by accident; he created you 'beautiful'. Believe it, anyone who does not agree with you on this, is the one with the problem and not you.

The adverse effects of worrying is so much that efforts must be made to overcome it. Apart from health problems, lack of charm and inability to see God's purpose for us, worrying can also make one to loose one's faith in God and worse still, become totally separated from God. Therefore, we must know how to deal with this cankerworm called 'worry'

1.   **Faith in God:** Absolute faith in God is the key to overcoming your anxiety knowing that God is still in control of that situation no matter how bad it seems. Remember that there is no new thing under the sun (Eccl 1 :9). That problem you have is not new, you are not the first to have it and certainly, you would not be the last. Exercise your faith in God through constant prayers If you spend half the time you waste on worrying on prayers, you would see the manifestation of God's power in your life. This is why the scriptures say, "*Be careful for nothing: but in everything by prayer and supplication with thanksgiving, let your requests be made known unto God. And the peace of God, which passeth all understanding, shall keep your hearts and mind through Christ Jesus*" (Phil 4:6-7). Worrying does not move God. Some people erroneously believe that when they weep, God will be moved to do something concerning their situation. They are wrong. It is our faith that moves God into action. Little wonder, the scriptures says '*without faith, it is impossible to please God*" (Hebrews 11:6).

2.   **Determination to Succeed:** Whatever it is that is giving you cause for worry, be determined to succeed concerning it. Whatever problem it is, be rest assured that it is not late. You can still excel where you thought you had failed. But if you give in to anxiety, you will not

have the strength to arise out of that situation. So what is it that you desire that is taking so long to materialize? Is it a job, children, spouse, good health or peace in your home? Do not give up. You can still make it. The problem with so many people is that they give up easily at the slightest delay or obstacle in the way. Do not quit, for quitters never win.

3.   **Encourage yourself**: Learn to encourage yourself instead of indulging in self-pity. It is also very un-wise to rely solely on other people to lift you up when you feel down. Everyone (without any exception) have their own peculiar problem, moreover no one can be with you all the time a good number of times you will find out that God is really the only one with you. Therefore, use the Word of God to minister good things to your 'spirit' and 'soul' when you feel 'down' or depressed. You can do this by knowing how to count your blessing, focus more on those things you already have instead of the things you think you lack. This in no way implies that you are to 'go it alone', avoiding or ignoring those who are in position to guide and encourage you when such is needed. Proverbs 27: 17 says, *"Iron sharpeneth iron: so a man sharpeneth the countenance of his friend"* therefore, you can seek the 'godly' counsel of 'God-fearing' ministers' of God, friends and family when led by the Holy Spirit. Be careful however not to seek counsel from individuals who would further compound your situation.

4.   **Study the Word:** The word of God is infallible and there is no problem in your life that the scriptures do not have an answer to: But what you do not know, you cannot apply therefore; you must make it a point of

duty to study the word at all times. Search the scripture for areas that deal with your situation, meditate on what the Lord is saying and pray with it. Such prayers will always receive quick response from God because the word of God is God himself(I *John* 1: 1), the enemy cannot hinder God. No wonder it is written that, *"For the word of God is quick and powerful and sharper than any two-edged sword, piercing to the dividing asunder of soul and spirit, and of joints and marrow, and is a discerner of the thoughts and intents of the heart"* (Heb 4:12). The word of God also builds up your faith and gives you the strength to continue instead of giving up.

5. **Constant fellowship with the brethren:** Has there been a time in your life when you came to church downcast but by the end of the service, you felt on top of the world. This is a 'recurring' testimony of most children of God. Therefore, it is absolutely wrong for you to neglect the gathering of the brethren because of a pressing need in your life that is yet to be met. *"But upon mount Zion, shall, be deliverance and holiness and the house of Jacob shall possess their possessions"* (Obadiah 1:17) this is what the Church represents. 'Zion' here refers to the house of God. Therefore, it is when you come to the house of God with the zeal to worship God in truth and in spirit so that you can have total deliverance from all your afflictions. Sitting down at home and complaining that the brethren have forsaken you would not solve your problem; go to 'Zion' and you will have all that you need.

6. **Thanksgiving:** A thankful heart is always a merry heart. You must cultivate the habit of showing appreciation

for whatever you are given, no matter how little. Say 'thank you' to God and the man or woman he uses to bless you. The problem with some people is that they are always waiting for the so-called 'big miracle' before they appreciate God. This should not be so. It is when you thank God for the 'little' that he would perform the big miracle for you. After all, you woke up this morning while many people did not. The fact that you are able to read this article is something to appreciate God for. Apart from God, also learn to appreciate everyone God uses to bless you every day, members of your family, colleagues, friends, pastor, church members e.t.c. Do not belittle any gift, appreciate it, and you would continue to receive more. Finally brethren, why worry when you can pray! Think about it.

WALKING BY FAITH

Apostle Paul bodly declared in 2 Cor. 5:7, *"For we walk by Faith, not by sight"*. This is a statement that appears so simple, yet very deep in meaning. Indeed, the apostles of old especially Paul actually walked by faith which enabled them to persevere in the face of diverse trials, temptations, difficulties and oppositions they encountered in the course of their ministries. This is why Paul was able to conclude in Rom. 8:38-39 *"For I am persuaded that neither death, nor life, nor angel, nor principalities, nor power. nor lift, nor things present, nor things to come, nor length, nor depth, nor any other creature, shall be able to separate us from the love of God, which is in Christ Jesus our Lord"*.

To walk by faith means to have absolute trust and believe in the Word of God and His promises. Heb. 11:1 says, *"Now faith is the substance of things hoped for, the evidence of things not seen "*. So when we say that we are walking by faith, we are saying that we do not have to see the immediate manifestation of answers to our prayers before we should believe that the Word of God is true and that it works.

The problem is that many of us want to see the physical manifestation of whatever we want God to do for us before believing. That is why some sick brethren even after they have been prayed for still continue to confess that they are sick. "You see, the pain is getting stronger and stronger. In fact, the situation was better before I came for prayer. It's like the moment I came for prayers, everything went haywires". Such people are walking by sight, they are looking for the physical manifestation, that is healing before they can believe that God heard their prayers; before they can believe that God can heal.

But when we walk by faith, our attitude should be: God says it, I believe it and that settles it". Whether you are seeing the immediate result or not, it shouldn't matter to you. Neither should it affect your believe in the power of God to fulfil His word. You believe that once God has promised anything, He is more than able to do it. Afterall, He assured us that *"My covenant will I not break, nor alte'r the things that is gone out of my lips,. Ps. 89:34.* What we need do, therefore, is to hold on tenaciously to the Word of God and then wait for the manifestation at God's appointed time Abraham was called the friend of God because he believed God. Of course it was imputed unto him for righteousness, Abraham believed despite the physical circumstances of his life and that of Sarah, his wife. Both were well advanced in years, past the age of children bearing. Abraham was 100 and Sarah, 90. Yet he did not consider his physical condition and the deadness of Sarah's womb, neither did he waver at the promise of God that he would father a child at his old age. Even when the promise did not come on time, he still held on to God's promise. *"And being not weak in faith, he considered not his own body now dead, when he was about hundred years old, neither yet the deadness of Sarah s womb. He staggered not at the promise of God through unbelief, but was strong in faith, giving glory to God. And being fully persuaded that what he had promised, he was able also to perform"* Rom. 4:1921.

The problem with us is that we look at our physical circumstances and years of waiting. It is not what we see that really matters. It is what God says in His word. We say "God has promised to prosper me financially but I have nothing doing. It is over five years I have left school now, I don't have a job. And I don't know anybody who can help me or give me money to start a business either. Yet God keeps telling me He will prosper me fmancially. I don't know how long I will keep waiting". "I have been married for five years now and all the people Who got married after me have children. God, why is my own case like this? What have I done? How long shall I continue to wait". "I am now 35 years old and I have been very faithfull to God since I gave my life to Christ. I have been paying tithe faithfully. I have been very committed and living a holy life. Yet, despite all these, no partner for me. God, how long shall I continue to pray? I am getting tired of waiting. I don't want to pray again, after all, what has happened since I have been praying? Many of us profess to believe the Word of God and His promises but we allow our physical senses, emotions, hmnan wisdom, oppositions, adversities to distract us. So in our hearts, we doubt the ability of God to perform His word in our lives. That is why inspite of confessing the word, we still go about complaining about our situations and our problems. And when the situation persists, we put the blame on either our enemies or the Pastor thinking that he does not have enough anointing to break the yoke in our lives. At times of course, some of us blame God for allowing sufferings and afflictions in our lives. *"But let him ask in faith, nothing wavering. For he that wavereth is like a wave of the sea driven with the wind and tossed For let not that man tMnk that he shall receive anything of the Lord"* Jam. 1 :67. Hence, many children of God go through life unfulfilled in certain areas where they could have excelled.

Walking by sight instead of faith

Son: Walking by sight instead of by faith. When we walk by sight, we tend to shift focus from God to man. We tend to depend on man for our victory and no longer on God. We tend to look to man for solutions to our problems. We see our fate as lying in the hands of man. We tend to see divine solutions as not coming on time, as being too slow. In short, we tend to be guided in our actions by our emotions, the opinion of man, human wisdom and not by the Word of God.

Another danger of walking by sight is that it leads to anxieties and fear which do not augur well for our physical and spiritual well-being. Fear robs man of victory. Satan uses fear to intimidate the children of God by magnifying a minor problem into a big obstacle in our minds and eyes. But when Satan tries to distract you with doubts and fear concerning the fulfilment of God's promise in your life and you stand on the Word of God to resist him and refuse to give up, he will have no option than to flee from you. Satan is not invincible. This is one thing many of us do not know. He may occasionally come with his problems such that your whole life appears to be heading for an end within minutes. But if you resist him steadfastly with the Words of God without taking side with him—by grumbling and complaining to God and confessing negative words—he will simply, leave you. _"Submit yourselves therefore to God. Resist the devil, and he willflee from you."_ James 4;7.

Had David been afraid of the huge size of Goliath, he would never have overpowered him. David knew his God and believed that with Him (God) on his side, victory was certain. Therefore, he was able to confidently declare the authority he had over Goliath in I Sam. 17:45 when he said _"Thou comest to me with a sword and a spew; and with a shield, but I come_ *to thee in the name of the Lord of hosts, the God of the armies of Israel, whom thou has defied"* And the result? He defeated Goliath and cut off the head of the Philistine giant who had terrorised the whole nation of Israel for long. No matter how bad our situation in life may seem to appear, when we walk by faith, they will not overwhelm us. In fact, walking by faith will lighten the weight of our problems as it means casting all our burdens at the feet of Jesus. The fourth verse of Chapter twenty-three of the book of Psalms will then have a deeper meaning for us. *"Yea, though I walk through the valley of the shadow of death, I will fiar no evil; fOr thou art with me; thy rod and thy staff they comfort me".* Thus our problems, adversities, afflictions will be seen as a passing moment, a testing period that will soon come to an end and catapult us to higher promotion, greater glory. Of course, we would, like Paul, (who inspite of the enormosity of his problems) say that all of them are nothing but little afflictions that cannot be compared with the glory that awaits us in eternity.

"For our light affliction, which is but for a moment, worketh for us a far more exceeding and eternal weight of glory. 2. Cor. 4: 17. If you must successfully walk by faith and not by sight, you must give yourself to the study of the Word, constantly meditate on the Word and pray ceaselessly.

We must also learn to be still in the face of trials and problems of life. Anxiety brings fear and a fearful man can hardly be victorious in any battle. Phil. 4:6-7 tells us to be *"careful for nothing, but in everything by prayer and supplication with thanksgiving, let your request be made known unto God. And the peace of God, which passeth, all understanding shall keep your hearts and minds through Christ Jesus".* What is that problem that is causing your faith to waver? Have you made your request to God by persistent prayers and thanksgiving? If so, why bother again?

Finally, you need patience if you are to walk by faith and not by sight. You should be able to endure, not easily discouraged or lose hope. This is because without these attributes in your life, your faith will begin to waver when you meet with delays in receiving answers to your prayers or having your needs met. It is impatience that makes some sisters decide to marry unbelievers in difiance of the Word of God. It is also impatience that makes some sisters looking for the fruits of the womb to go to fetish priests and false prophets. *"For ye have need of patience that after ye have done the will of God, ye might receive the promise"* Heb. 10:36. Brethren, as we await the coming of our Lord Jesus Christ, we cannot but walk by faith. This is because if we do not in the face of difficulties and challenges of this present world, we may not found it easy abiding in the Christian race till He comes.

THE UNKNOWN ENEMY

Many people shudder at the mere thought of the word 'enemy'. Whether we like it or not. as children of God. We would always have at least one enemy, SATAN. But in this article. we are more concerned about the unknown enemy, who could even be your close friend. a neighbor, colleague. a member of your family. Brethren, it is a very dangerous situation to have as an enemy someone you are very close to, a confidant. At least a known enemy can be avoided. handled but an unknown one can create a lot of havoc before you are even aware of his/her existence. No wonder Hosea 4:6 says "My people are destroyed for lack of knowledge".

As human beings. we do not have the natural ability to recognize an enemy, except those who have exposed themselves to us in words or actions. There had been cases of people pretending to be good friends, confidants to others, only to turn out to be their foes. It takes the grace and mercy of God to recognize such people because they portray an outward appearance of warmness towards the ones they hate. Only God knows what is in the heart of men. «The heart is deceitful above all things and desperately wicked who can know it" Jer.17:9.

The easiest foe to handle is the one you know such as the devil and his agents. This is because the scripture has given us the guidelines of dealing with them "Submit yourselves therefore to God, resist the devil and he will flee from you" James 4:7. But the most dangerous foe is the one who eats with you, laughs with you, and yet devises ways to plot your downfall. This is why we should always pray to God to expose unfriendly friends and severe our relationship with them. To be nonchalant, because you have not seen any visible sign of enmity from anyone can lead to a lot of temptation.

The unknown enemy can come in several ways:

- It could be that close friend whom you trust so much and confide in. Many relationships, marriages have been ruined by so called "trusted" friends who turned out to be enemies in disguise "faithful are the wounds of a friend but the kisses of an enemy are deceitful" Prov. 27:6. It is good to have friends; they add value to our lives. But we must be very careful and prayerful in the choice of our friends. For our closest associations can make or mar our destiny. Therefore you must pray to God to give you God fearing and sincere friends, and to separate those that are not of Him from your life. Believe it or not, until you let go of some close associates you may never accomplish your desired goals.

  Some people may not possess evil powers, but have used their mouths to create havoc in the lives of their so-called friends; they reveal intimate secrets of their friends to others creating conflicts in their relationships. They deliberately spread tales about their friends in order to pull them down, because secretly they envy them for one reason or the another. No wonder Proverb 16:28 states that "A forward man soweth strife and a whisperer separateth chief friends".

- Your unknown enemy could also be that your colleague in the office, business partner who openly admires you for your intelligence and dedication to duty; but secretly devises means to displace you from your enviable position.

There have been cases where some even try to use diabolic means to kill one another. In today's competitive world, there are so many intrigues in the corporate and business environment. This is why we must be prayerful and apply wisdom in our relationship with anyone directly or indirectly involved in our source of income. The Lord commanded us to work in order to eat (2nd Thess 3:10). Therefore we must protect our means of livelihood, not allowing the enemy to take it away from us.

• Your unknown enemy could also be that your 'nice' neighbor whom you constantly gossip with, narrating all that is happening in your household. Before you realize it, your once peaceful home is turned into a battleground. "A man that beareth false witness against his neighbor is a maul and a sword and a sharp arrow" Prov. 25:18

• Believe it or not, members of your own family could also be the unknown enemy in your life. "For the son dishonoureth the father, the daughter riseth up against her mother, the daughter-in-law against her mother-in-law, a man's enemies are the men of his own house" Micah 7:6. We know we cannot change the family we are born into, but when the source of a problem is traced to anyone within the family, it makes the situation easier to handle. After all, a problem known is half solved; a disease that has been correctly diagnosed is easier to treat than undiagnosed illness. There had been cases where parents were even responsible for their children's predicaments.

In a nutshell, the unknown enemy could be anybody, even the least expected. It is only God who knows the heart of men towards us.

"for the Lord searcheth all hearts and understandeth all the imaginations of the thought" (I Chron 28:9).

HOW TO IDENTIFY THE UNKNOWN ENEMY

Before you jump into the conclusion that the man/woman you had a misunderstanding with yesterday is your unknown enemy, it is pertinent to realize that as long as we live there would always be little conflict in relationships; but not all result in enmity. In fact the one that is indeed your enemy, maybe the person who had never even disagreed with you.

The following can go a long way in helping us to identify any unknown enemy in our lives.

PRAYER can expose your enemy. "Pray that ye enter not into temptation" Luke 22:40. One of your consistent prayer points should be that the Lord should reveal the source of any problem in your life; and that he should expose any unknown enemy to you. Brethren, there are some friends, associates that you have to separate from before you accomplish your goals. Lot had to be separated from Abraham before Abraham could enter into God's glorious destiny for him (Gen 13:7-9).

ASK FOR THE SPIRIT OF DISCERNMENT:

To live a successful Christian life, we need the spirit of discernment "But strong meat belongeth to them that are of full age, even those who by reason of use have their senses exercised to discern both good and evil" Heb 5: 14. To live in the flesh all the time in this evil world spells doom for any believer. Some Christians erroneously believe that it is only Pastors and Ministers of God that need this gift of discernment in the performance of their pastoral duties. The truth is that, every born again child of God who desires the gift of the Spirit can have them "Now there are diversities of gifts but the same Spirit" (I Cor 12:4) "To another the working of miracle; to another prophecy; to another discerning of spirit; to another divers kinds of tongues; to another interpretation of tongues" I Cor 12:10.

GIFTS OF REVELATION:

This gift can be exercised in various ways by the Holy Spirit through the word of knowledge, word of wisdom, dreams or visions. But the extent to which you can obtain and utilize them will depend on your relationship with God. You must be a committed Christian, prayerful, constantly meditating on the word of God. What you do not have, you cannot use. It is the word of God, and the Spirit of God within you, that will reveal your enemies and even their plans to you.

A word of caution here: It is not every dream that emanates from God. The devil can also manipulate dreams; therefore you must be sure of your right standing with God and the ways he reveals things to you personally in order not to create confusion and unnecessary enemies in life. Go is not a respecter of anyone; whoever desires his spiritual gifts is given as long as he has given his life fully to him

"All that time Jesus answered and said, I thank thee, o father, Lord of heaven and earth, because thou host hid these things from the wise and prudent, and host revealed unto babes!" Matt II :25

CONCLUSION

Brethren, we know that only God can save us from our enemies, but we do not have to wait to see their manifestations in our lives before we take necessary actions. The three wise men from the east were warned in a dream not to go back to king Herod after presenting their gifts to the infant Jesus. "And being warned of God in a dream that they should not return to Herod, they deported into their own country another way (easy)'", Matt 2: 12. The Lord is still in the business of revealing our enemies to us. He has not changed, but we must have a close and committed relationship with Him, for He only reveals secrets to His children. Shalom!

A SOLID FOUNDATION

The foundation of anything is very important; be It your house, marriage, career, relationships, Christianity and even your life. No wonder the word of God says "If the foundation be destroyed, what can the righteous do?" (Ps 11 :3). If most of us would be honest with ourselves, we would discover that the root of some of the problems we are experiencing in certain areas of our lives is as a result of a faulty or—shaky foundation. You only have to go to a building site to witness the expertise involved and the pains taken in laying the foundation of any building, and then you would realize the essence of a good foundation in every area of our lives. This is why our Lord Jesus Christ likened the one who 'hearest' his sayings and 'doeth' them to a man who built his house upon a rock "And the rain descended and the flood came, and the wind blew and beat upon that house: and it fell not: for it was founded upon a rock" (Matt 7 :25). And as for the man who heareth his words and refused to do them, he likened him to a foolish man who built. his house upon the sand: "And the rain descended, and the flood came, and the winds blew and beat upon that house, and it fell: and great was the fall of it" (Matt 7:2'7). Would you rather be like the wise man or foolish one? The choice is yours. Many marriages, careers, relationships are in jeopardy today because the people involved were more concerned with what they could gain at the beginning than focusing on how to make a success of it. Therefore, at the slightest problem or temptation, they succumb to the devices of the enemy. They then begin to run from pillar to post looking for solutions to their problems instead of enjoying the blessing God had given to them. Be wise; in your relationships, career and marriage, be committed to laying a solid foundation that cannot be destroyed no matter the devices of the devil; and built upon it with help of the Lord (He is the master builder).

LIFE

Have you ever tried to' assess the foundation of your life? Many lives have been turned upside down today as a result of what happened before, during or after their birth. Past activities of parents, families and even the place of birth have been known to be responsible for certain problems faced by people, even children of God. Ignorance of this fact has led to so much frustration in many lives. No wonder Hosea 4:6 says: "My people are destroyed for lack of knowledge". A problem known is half-solved. But you should not stop at knowing the problem; something must be done to remedy it. We may not be able to influence the foundation of our lives, but we have the liberty to ask the Lord to revisit our foundation to repair, restore what has been distorted or destroyed. Do not leave things to chance, probe into the past deeds and misdeeds of your family, parents and ancestors. Try. to ascertain if there is a correlation with your present predicament, then hand over the past, present and the future to God who is able to rebuild and reconstruct your life. You do not have to be a partaker of the affliction of your ancestors; the blood of Jesus was shed to free us from all condemnation: "There is therefore now no condemnation to them which are in Christ Jesus, who walk not after the flesh but after the Spirit" (Rom 8: 1). You should therefore renounce and repent of every evil covenant operating in your life either inherited or self-induced. Failure to do so may lead to years of frustration and untold hardship instead of enjoying the blessings of God.

MARRIAGE

The foundation of every marriage should be God and genuine love. "Except the Lord build the house, they labor in vain that build it: except the Lord keeps the city, the watchman waketh but in vain" (Psalm 127:1). If you are already married, honestly assess the foundation on which your marriage was based. If the foundation of your marriage was faulty, do not despair, there is still room for God's mercy to prevail. Your own part is to be honest with yourself and be committed to correcting your mistakes. This can only be done by surrendering your marriage to God and being obedient to his instructions.

For the unmarried, you are privileged to know that there is no substitute to laying a solid foundation for your marriage. Some marriages are troubled today because the couples involved got into the marriage just to satisfy their desires. Money, beauty, educational qualifications, tribal or family background and other ephemeral features were considered to be of more importance than ascertaining whether it was God's will or not. In some cases, love was totally absent, while others confused lust for love. A marriage based on one or more ephemeral factors alone will not stand, there must be genuine love and God's approval, for He is the author of the marriage institution. Gen 2:24 says "Therefore shall a man leave his father and his mother and shall cleave unto his wife and the two shall be one flesh". The mistake some people make is that they make their own choice and then ask God to bless the union. They deliberately leave God out of the process of choosing a spouse only to come running to him when the trial begins.

Little wonder they are easily overwhelmed by simple marital disputes. It is true that there is no marriage without its own minor problems, but if God is in it from the beginning, no situation will succeed in destroying that marriage. On the other hand however, minor problems can succeed in breaking some marriages that are not built on God's will. Trials in marriages are supposed to bring couples closer and not to separate them.

CAREER

"Whatever thy hand findeth to do, do it with thy might..." (Ecc 9: l0a). But what do we find today? Many people see their jobs merely as a meal ticket. It is true that the primary objective of having a career is for the material gains accruable, but like in other aspects of life you must aim to make a success of it. As long as what you are doing is not criminal or evil, it is your duty to lay a solid foundation and build upon it. Many people dream of being at the helm of affairs of their company, but are not prepared to work their way through to the top. Wishing alone will not make your dream a reality. You must start from now, to lay a solid foundation through hard work, commitment to service, honesty and determination to succeed. "Seest thou a man diligent in his business? He shall stand before kings: he shall not stand before mean men" (Proverbs 22:29).

It is wrong to think that your human connections alone will take you to the top of your career. Take a survey of some chief executives of big companies or banks and you would discover that most of them did not get to their present position based on 'connections' alone, their ability to perform, hard work was more likely to have led to their successes. Even if you get to the top by crooked means, you may not last there because your foundation was faulty.

It is the foundation that you lay at the beginning of your career that you built upon. So many businesses do not succeed because the owners started them on a wrong footing. If you use 'stolen' money to establish a business, it is bound to fail. In the same way, if you set up a business without proper planning and knowledge of such a business you may run into big problems because the foundation was shaky. Know what you want to do, do proper research, plan and above all seek God's approval before going into any business venture.

RELATIONSHIPS

There are different types of relationships. Here, we would confine ourselves to friendship between people of the same sex, opposite sex and even courtship. You would be surprised to know that today, many people cultivate the friendship of others, not based on mutual interest or likeness as it used to be, but more on what the other person possess that would be beneficial to them. Money, position in the society, human connections have become the basis of friendships for some people even members of the church. Friendship has become a tool of manipulation for certain people. They cultivate the friendship of specific people because they believe they have a lot to gain from them.

Invariably such; so-called' relationship crumbles because the other person would one day, discover that he or she has been set up to be 'used'. And we all know that no human being would like to be 'used' by anyone. Everyone wants to be loved and respected for who they are and not for what they have. This is why so many people cherish childhood friends, people who knew them when they were 'nobody' and are still around them. "A man loveth at all times" (Proverbs 17: 17a).

Examine yourself, do you always cultivate friendship that don't last? Probably, the fault is yours. It is good to have good friends, but you should never forget that it is a give-and-take situation. Be a true friend to others, and you would have great friends. "A man that hath friends must show himself friendly; and there is a friend that sticketh closer than a brother" (Proverbs 18:24).

CHRISTIANITY

Is your zeal to serve God always increasing and decreasing in succession? Since you gave your life to Christ has it become a habit for you to constantly re-dedicate your life to God because of your constant trend of backsliding? If this is the situation, you must sit down and assess the foundation of your Christian life. How did you come to the Lord? Was it because you had a problem and someone told you told you that coming to church would solve it? Was it that your friends had all given their lives to Christ and you did not want to be the odd one out? Or was it that you had the impression that coming to church would enable you to get a good husband/wife. Even if it was a need that brought you to the Lord, you must first of all repent genuinely, serve him faithfully and then he would give you more than you asked for. "But seek ye first the kingdom of God and its righteousness and all these things shall be added unto you" (Matthew 6:33). It is only a fool that keeps coming to the Lord and going back to the world (old evil habits). The scriptures say that such a person is not fit for the kingdom of God (Luke 9:62). Lay a solid foundation for your Christianity, be rooted and grounded in the word of God and no amount of trial or temptation will be able to separate you from the Lord (Rom 8:35-38).

REQUIREMENTS FOR A SOLID FOUNDATION

1. **God's Approval:** It is needless embarking on any endeavor in life without God's approval. For you to have a successful marriage, career or relationships, the foundation must be on the Lord. "For no other foundation can any man lay than that that is laid, which is Jesus Christ." (1 Corinthians 3: 11). Many people have gone into marriages and businesses without God's approval, only to remember God when troubles threaten to overwhelm them. Be wise, do not take any important decision or embark on any worthy venture without seeking the face of the Lord, abiding by whatever decision He takes even if it is not to your liking. Remember, "Except the Lord builds the house, they labour in vain that build it: except the Lord keep the city, the watchman waketh but in vain". (Psalm 127:1).

2. **Patience:** This is a pre-requisite for a solid foundation. Laying a solid foundation in any area of life is usually accompanied with so much trials and temptations that without patience, one is likely to give up. No wonder the scripture says:

    "Therefore thus saith the Lord God, Behold I lay in Zion for a foundation a stone, a tried stone, a precious comer stone, a sure foundation: he that believeth shall not make haste" (Isa 28:16). You cannot run before you can walk therefore, you must be patient in that your marriage, job, relationship, or business, everything cannot be perfect at once. You should be able to endure some of the unpalatable things that will happen as you strive to make a success of it. Even when you are doing the right things, some people will still oppose you. On your job, some people will hate you for refusing to join in their corruption. Do not allow the opinion of others to dissuade you from doing the right thing. Some would even persecute you for not towing the line of the world to get things done at all cost, even when it is not of God, but remember the scripture says, "For you have need of patience that after ye have done the will of God, ye might receive the promise"(Heb 1 0:36).

3. **Focus:** So many people stumble and fail in life due to lack of focus. What do you really want? Are you going into that relationship, marriage or career to make a success of it or is it because it is what is expected of you? When your eyes are focused on where you are going or where you want to be, nothing will deter you from reaching your goal. The task at hand may seem so difficult now, do not give up. Remember, we are told to walk by faith, not by sight. (2 Corinthians 5:7). If you are easily distracted or overwhelmed by problems, you cannot lay a good foundation. Focus on what you aim to achieve and on God who will make it possible.

BENEFITS OF A SOLID FOUNDATION

Every sane human being would actually want to succeed in every aspect of life. But the problem lies with our innate abilities to work towards success. Success does not just happen; you have to make it happen. The Lord is committed to blessing our efforts because he said our labor would not be in vain. (Isa 65:21-22)—"And they shall build houses and inhabit them: and they shall not plant and another eat: for as the days of a tree are the days of my people, and mine elect shall long enjoy the work of their hands". Some of these great benefits inc1ude:-

(a) **Success where others fail:**—Is it not wonderful to see a couple celebrating their silver or golden jubilee wedding anniversary and still radiating the love they share? The foundation was laid years ago. Would you like to have friends who would stick to you no matter the situation? Your own attitude towards friendship would determine that. Would you love to succeed in business that others say is not viable? If the Lord had approved it and you obediently allowed him to guide you, then you would be the envy of others due to your success.

(b) **Honor:**—This can come in various dimensions, even from the unexpected quarters. Workers are honored periodically for diligence and honesty in the discharge of their duties. This can come in form of promotions or cash awards. Before they realize it, they have moved ahead far above their contemporaries.

(c) **Sense of fulfillment:**—Above all, it is everyone's desire to be fulfilled in every area of life physically, spiritually, financially, and maritially. This is possible because with God, all things are possible. But you have an important part to play. Lay a solid foundation. Do not be in a hurry to reap, when you have not sown. In your relationships, marriage, career and spiritual life, sow good seeds, work hard and surrender all to God; the result will surpass even your great expectations. Shalom!

THE TRUE WISDOM

Some people think they are wise because they have the ability to manipulate others to get whatever they want, while others believe they are wise because their wrong doings are yet to be exposed. We should bear in mind that God sees everything; "For nothing is secret that shall not be made manifest, neither is anything hid, that shall not be known and come abroad" Luke 8:17. In the same vein, there is still another group of people who think they are wise because their reliance and use of occultic powers have yielded some success. This type of success will not last; whatever success you have achieved that is not of God will never last. Any power contrary to God's power is deceptive. For the scripture clearly states in Psalm 62: 11 that "God hath spoken once, twice have I heard this, that power belongeth unto God."

WHAT IS THE TRUE WISDOM?

True wisdom is the wisdom that is from God. This type of wisdom is described in James 3: 17 as pure, then peaceable, gentle and easy to be entreated, full of mercy and good fruits, without partiality and without hypocrisy. We need a measure of this type of wisdom in every aspect of our lives. The more you have of it, the more success you will record in life. The non-availability of God's wisdom in your life can lead to frustration and mediocrity; which means that you may even find it difficult to succeed in the simplest things. No wonder the word of God says in Prov. 4:7 "Wisdom is the principal thing; therefore get wisdom and with all thy getting, get understanding."

We might be wondering how to get hold of this kind of wisdom. The wisdom of God is contained in His book, called the 'Holy Bible.' There is no need or situation in our lives that God has not made provision for in the scriptures. By consistently dwelling on the word of God, you will be able to discover the hidden wisdom of God needed to excel in every area of life. Joshua 1:8 states thus: "This book of the law shall not depart out of thy mouth, but thou shalt meditate therein day and night, that thou mayest observe to do ~ according to all that is written therein: for then thou shalt make thy way prosperous, and then/ thou shalt have good success."

We can also receive this type of wisdom by asking from God. For the scripture says, "If any of you ill lack wisdom, let him ask of God, that giveth to all men liberally, and upbraidth not: and it shall be given him. (James 1.5).

Below is an expose on the need for wisdom in two important aspects of our lives—The home and business.

WISDOM IN THE HOME

Most people are of the view that the essential requirement for a happy home is for God to bless them with a good life partner, wonderful children and enough resources to cater for them. It is not enough to have the above more importantly, you need the wisdom of God to make your home the way God created it to be. You cannot rely on your intelligence and financial resources alone to make your home peaceable. The whole money in the world cannot buy peace for your home.

You need wisdom in your relationship with your spouse, children, in-laws, neighbors and friends, because whether you like it or not, these groups of people can affect your home in one way or the other. Failure in your dealings with one group can negatively affect the others. For instance, a wife's poor relationship with her in-laws can lead to a strain in her marriage. Since the wisdom of God is in His word, therefore as a husband or a wife, you must locate the relevant portions in the bible relating to your duties and obligations. It is not enough to know the word, we must also practise it in our daily lives. To do this, we need the grace of God. This is why we must pray ceaselessly for ourselves and every members of our family.

For instance, it is imperative that every wife must know that the wisdom of God says she must be submissive to her husband, (Eph 5:22). Similarly, every husband must know that it is important he loves his wife just as Christ loved the church (Eph 5:25). Anything contrary to this will mean that a couple is not operating in the wisdom of Gad}. This has often led to a lot of conflicts in many homes. It is therefore not surprising that the scripture says in Prov. 24:3-4:

"Through wisdom is an house builded and by understanding it is established: And by knowledge shall the chambers be filled with all precious and pleasant riches.

The wife as a homemaker, should exceptionally ask for the wisdom of God in order to build her home. She needs wisdom particularly in her relationship with her children and in-laws. She should never be too busy with her job or business or become too modern in her ways to correct her children, for this may later affect her marriage: "A wise son maketh a glad father: but a foolish son is the heaviness of his mother." (Prov.

10:1). In the same way, a wise woman must also be discrete in her dealings with her in-laws, especially her husband's parents. She must realise that despite the fact her husband has left his father and mother to cleave unto her according to divine injunction it does not mean that he has ceased to be a member of his family, or that his responsibility towards his parents has stopped. Therefore, a wise woman should try her best in whatever way she can, to assist her husband in discharging his duties towards his parents, morally or financially instead of dissuading her husband from helping his parents as some women may want to do. By so doing, she will be laying a good foundation for her marriage and her children. Remember God's warning in Prov. 14:1 which says; "Every wise woman buildeth her house: but the foolish plucketh it down with her hands." So seek and ask for the wisdom of God today to enable you be a builder of your home and not to spoil it.

WISDOM IN BUSINESS.

Do you know that the wisdom of God is an essential ingredient for financial prosperity in your business?

Some people erroneously believe that all they require to start a good business is enough capital. You can have all the money you need and even more, however, if you lack wisdom, the business may not succeed. This is why you see some people going into a particular business but in the end, they have nothing to show for it. This will not be your portion in Jesus Name, Amen.

If you belong to the above category or currently your business is not making headway, pause now and examine yourself. Have you relied solely on your human intelligence and your resources, without applying the wisdom of God in your business? If yes, this is the time to retrace your steps and diligently seek God's word as it concerns your business and prosperity.

Prov. 8: 12 says, "I, Wisdom dwell with prudence, and find out knowledge of witty inventions." Therefore, have you been prudent in spending your money or do you just invest money without doing a proper feasibility study of what you are investing your money on? Do you actually have a deep knowledge of the kind of business you are into? The problem with many people is that they like to go into any business that is in vogue, even when they know little or nothing about it. You can choose to establish a business that will suit you and also bring in the desired financial 'rewards. However, make sure you ask for wisdom to help you think of new business ideas that others will look up to tomorrow.

Another aspect where wisdom is very essential in business is in the location of any type of business, no matter how big or small. For instance, a couple of years ago, a young lady opened a big supermarket with a lot of fanfare, in a very quiet street with few houses and very few pedestrians and cars passing through. Therefore, many people were not even aware of the existence of the supermarket. After a short while, she became discouraged because there were hardly enough sales to pay her workers salaries, not to talk of replenishing her stock. Eventually she had to move to more favorable location with the little stock she had remaining. It is obvious that she did not apply wisdom in her choice of location for her supermarket, otherwise she would have realized that, the former location was not suitable for a supermarket of that magnitude.

This is what true wisdom is all about. It will make you succeed where others fail. It will amaze those around you as they began to see the wonderful works of God in your life. So ask for wisdom from God today and do not just stop there, seek diligently for it in the WORD of God, which has been made readily available for you. SHALOM!